CW00485318

JANE'S DELICIOUS KITCHEN

June 2012

Dear Simon and Sarah,

Enjoy making the most of your harvest!

Jane

Harvesting, preserving and cooking seasonal food

JANE GRIFFITHS

Photographs by Keith Knowlton and Jane Griffiths

SUNBIRD PUBLISHERS

The illustrated imprint of Jonathan Ball Publishers

First published in 2010
Reprinted in 2011
Sunbird Publishers (Pty) Ltd
PO Box 6836
Roggebaai 8012
Cape Town, South Africa

www.sunbirdpublishers.co.za

Registration number: 1984/003543/07

Copyright published edition © Sunbird Publishers
Copyright text © Jane Griffiths
Copyright images © Jane Griffiths

www.janesdeliciousgarden.com

Design and typesetting by MR Design
Cover design by MR Design
Editing and project management by Michelle Marlin
Photographs by Jane Griffiths and Keith Knowlton
Publisher Ceri Prenter
Printed and bound by Tien Wah Press Pte Ltd (Singapore)

Jane Griffiths asserts the moral right to be identified as the author of this work. All rights reserved. No part of this publication may be reproduced, stored in a retrieval system or transmitted, in any form or by means, electronic, mechanical, photocopying, recording or otherwise, without prior written permission of the copyright owner(s).

ISBN 978-1-920289-15-7

While every last effort has been made to check that information in this recipe book is correct at the time of going to press, the publisher, author and their agents will not be held liable for any damages incurred through any inaccuracies.

Thanks to Lulu Bailey from Lucky Fish and Adriaan Turgel from Liebermann Pottery for letting me pick and choose from their wonderful selection of tableware.

There is enough for all.
The earth is a generous mother;
she will provide in plentiful abundance
food for all her children
if they will but cultivate her soil
in justice and in peace.
Bourke Coekran

For Keith – who eats my experiments with gusto

Thanks to:
My friends – you all know I love feeding you;
Karen for suggesting I should write my recipes down;
Ceri, Michelle and Marius for steering the second ship safely into port;
and most of all to Mom, who taught me to be adventurous.

CONTENTS

INTRODUCTION

When Keith and I first met, he did all the cooking. I could throw together a few basics, but Keith produced complex curries and mouth-watering pastas. My taste buds were onto a good thing and stayed out of the kitchen.

In 1991 we spent a couple of months in Thailand and, after that, everything changed. I came back hankering after the fresh tastes and fiery combinations I had been relishing. Armed with my birthday present from Keith, Charmaine Solomon's *South East Asian Cooking*, I made long lists of unfamiliar ingredients. Forays into Fordsburg's Indian spice dens and Commissioner Street's Chinese supermarkets followed. My addiction to cooking and collecting ingredients had begun.

In the months and years that followed, I travelled to many countries. My pantry soon overflowed with delicious-smelling spices and pastes. My sketchbooks filled with scribbled techniques and colourful sketches of exotic fare. Each month the post box would explode with foodie magazines from all corners of the globe and Charmaine Solomon was joined on the bookshelf by many more authors. And so I learned to cook.

My friends and family were my guinea pigs. If I was going to make a complicated dish, I was going to do it only once. I wasn't going to waste time practising – if it didn't work, so what? And most often, my experiments did work. Well, there were a few that backfired, like my first spinach and ricotta ravioli. The filling was delicious and the handmade pasta superb. But I missed the bit where I was meant to dust the freshly made ravioli with flour and keep them separated until dry. The resulting ravioli mountain scored zero for presentation.

I have travelled to many places, but my favourite journey is the one from my kitchen door to my vegetable garden. With a colander and a pair of scissors, the evening meal is decided by whatever is freshest and most enticing. To make and eat a meal of freshly picked ingredients is immensely satisfying, empowering and delicious. It is also one of the healthiest ways to eat, both for our planet and for us. The journey from your kitchen to your vegetable garden leaves no carbon footprint.

Even if you don't grow your own food, *Jane's Delicious Kitchen* will help you make the most of what is in season. It is about cooking fresh food and harvesting, preserving and storing the abundance.

CREATIVE COOKING

My first book, *Jane's Delicious Garden*, was about how to grow organic vegetables and herbs. This book is about how to eat them. But this does not mean you need to grow your own organic vegetables in order to use this book. Although I don't specify it in the following recipes, I do recommend you use as many organic and free-range ingredients as you can. And that you choose fresh, seasonal ingredients whenever possible. Find out where the nearest organic farmers' market is and make the effort to support it. You will certainly taste the difference.

I have never done a cooking course nor been to a cookery school. Everything I have learnt about cooking has been through trial and error, observation, tasting and reading. I can throw an Asian dish together within half an hour – but I get nervous at the thought of cooking a lamb roast. So I am not an expert chef by any means. However, as with my gardening methods, I have worked out many short cuts. Only occasionally will I prepare something that takes hours of my devoted time. Most often I decide what to cook only about half an hour before we sit down to eat whatever it is I have concocted.

I very seldom follow a recipe exactly. I tend to use it as an inspiration and a guide, adding a dash of this or a pinch of that to suit my taste. Often I don't have the exact ingredients in my pantry, which leads to improvising and adapting the recipe to make the most of what I do have. And therein lies the joy of cooking: once you make the leap and begin experimenting, it becomes a creative and absorbing process, not merely making something to eat. Different senses come into play – how does it smell, what does it look like, how does it feel? Often I don't taste a dish until right at the end, rather relying on my sense of smell to guide me until I make final adjustments according to taste. Or I will add a specific ingredient just because of its colour. I daydream about combinations of flavours, imagining how they will taste together. And so, at the end of a busy day, I find that I relax by preparing a meal. Cooking should not be a chore; it should be an inspiring, inventive and uplifting source of pleasure.

Above all, approach your cooking with a sense of adventure. Don't be afraid of experimenting, even if you are having guests for dinner. Remember, if everything does go belly up, you can always order take-aways.

When baking,
follow directions.
When cooking, go by
your own taste.
Laiko Bahrs

SEPTEMBER 22 – DECEMBER 21

*I love spring anywhere, but if I could choose
I would always greet it in a garden.*
Ruth Stout

Spring is the time to be busy after the hibernation of winter. The garden is unfurling, green and new, with a freshly awakened sense of discovery. It is time to box up the woollies and stretch away winter by delving into a spring garden. At the beginning of spring I am always seduced by the promise of the inviting space. By the end of spring I usually have way too many plants, which have to be thinned, trimmed and transplanted.

IN SEASON IN SPRING

Artichokes	Lettuces	Rocket
Asian greens	Nasturtiums	Spinach
Asparagus	Onions	Spring herbs
California poppies	Pansies	Spring onions
Coriander	Parsley	Strawberries
Cornflowers	Peas	Swiss chard
Garlic	Plums	
Leeks	Radishes	

SPRING

ARTICHOKES

Although you can mess around with artichokes by baking and stuffing them, I much prefer the simplest method of eating them. It's like carefully opening a lovingly wrapped present. Start by peeling off the outer leaves one by one, dip them in lemon butter and then scrape the fleshy base off with your teeth. The outer leaves have only a slim edible portion, but as you work your way closer to the centre, the fleshier they become, until you arrive at the delectable heart of the artichoke. Take care to pull off the cluster of fluffy hairs in the centre before eating the heart.

Artichokes hold a further surprise – they are perfect paired with what I call Mother's Milk (because it is my mother's cocktail of choice: a tot of whisky and an ice cube in half a glass of milk). There is something about artichokes that plays on the taste buds and makes milk taste heavenly sweet.

Harvesting, buying and storing artichokes

In early October the central bud will begin ripening, followed by smaller side buds. Cut the buds while they are still firm, with the leaves tightly closed. Cut the stem about 3 cm to 5 cm below the base of the bud. If left on the plant, they will open into beautiful (but inedible) thistle-like flowers.

When buying artichokes, look for ones that are tightly closed and heavy in relation to their size. Artichokes keep quite well in the fridge or on a cool veggie rack for up to two weeks.

Pasta Vetrina with lemony artichoke sauce

Embedded with fresh green herbs, this 'wow' translucent pasta looks marvellous but is deceptively simple to make.

It really helps to have a pasta machine, but if you want to give it a bash using a rolling pin, go for it – although the pasta sheets will end up slightly thicker. I like using coriander and parsley. Not only do they taste good, the leaves create a pretty pattern. Try using tarragon or dill as a variation.

PASTA

- 500 g flour
- 5 large eggs
- 1 cup mixed flat leaf parsley and coriander leaves, washed and dried
- semolina flour for dusting

SERVES 4

PASTA

Place the flour on a work surface and make a well in the centre. Break the eggs into the well and, using a fork, stir them gently, incorporating flour from the sides. As soon as the mixture starts coming together as dough, start using your hands. Knead the dough for about 3 minutes, until it is smooth and elastic. Wrap in cling wrap, and leave in the fridge for an hour.

Divide the chilled dough into 4 pieces and roll them into balls. Cover 3 of them in cling wrap and put them back in the fridge. Set the rollers of your pasta machine to the widest setting. Flatten the dough ball slightly with your hand to create a rectangle, and run it through the machine. Then turn the dial down one notch and feed it through. Turn the notch back up to the widest setting, fold the dough in half and feed it through the rollers again.

Repeat this rolling and folding through the top two settings 3 to 4 more times. If it starts sticking, dust with a little flour. This rolling and folding works the dough and makes it smooth and elastic.

To thin out the pasta, turn the dial down a notch and feed the dough through again. Continue turning the dial down until the pasta has gone through the thinnest setting. Your dough should be one long strip about 1 to 1.5 mm thin but if it has broken into pieces, don't worry. Hang them over the back of a chair so they don't stick to one another and adapt the following instructions.

Cut the long strip into two equal lengths and lay them flat on a work surface. Cover half of each length with fresh herb leaves – don't just scatter them, place them so they create a pattern. Fold the other half of the strip over the top and gently press down to seal it. Carefully run the herbed strips through the pasta machine to seal the two layers together. Cut the sheets into lasagne-sized

squares and dust very lightly with semolina flour to prevent them from sticking. Place the herbed squares on a baking tray lined with baking paper, keeping them separate until they have dried slightly. Repeat the entire process with the other 3 dough balls. You should end up with about 32 squares. If you don't cook them immediately, let them dry completely and store in zip lock bags.

Cook in salted, boiling water with a splash of olive oil for about 4 minutes.

LEMONY ARTICHOKE SAUCE
Cook the artichokes according to the recipe on page 17. Once they are cool enough to handle, remove the leaves, scraping off the edible flesh from the base

using a teaspoon. When you reach the artichoke heart, remove the hairs from the surface and discard them. Clean off any hard sections from the base and cut the hearts into chunks.

In a medium-sized saucepan, melt the butter over medium heat. Add the spring onions and sauté until just softened. Add the salt, chilli powder and a few grinds of pepper. Stir through until blended. Add the flour to the butter and onion mixture, stirring until well mixed and cook for a couple of minutes until it starts to turn golden.

Remove from the heat and slowly add the milk, stirring all the time to make sure no lumps form. Return to the heat and bring to the boil, stirring regularly, until it begins to thicken. Add the lemon juice, whisking it in quickly. Add the prepared artichoke flesh and hearts. As soon as the sauce comes to a simmer, add the chilli strips and remove from the heat. Season to taste with salt and freshly ground pepper. Serve over the herb pasta topped with sprinklings of fresh parsley.

LEMONY ARTICHOKE SAUCE
- 12 large artichokes
- 4 tablespoons butter
- 8 spring onions, sliced
- 1 teaspoon salt
- pinch chilli powder
- freshly ground pepper
- 2 tablespoons flour
- 2 cups milk
- 2 tablespoons lemon juice
- mild red chilli, cut into thin strips
- flaked sea salt and black pepper
- fresh parsley, chopped

SERVES 4

Artichokes with lemon butter

Although lemon butter is a classic combination with artichokes, try making some chilli and garlic butter too. Don't forget to put a big bowl on the table for all the discarded leaves.

Rinse 8 artichokes under cold running water. Cut the stems to about 3 cm. Fill a large pot with water and bring it to the boil. Place the artichokes in the pot, ensuring they are covered. Reduce heat to a simmer. Cover the pot and cook for 30 to 40 minutes. While they are cooking, make the lemon butter.

Test the artichokes for readiness by pulling off the outer leaves with tongs. When they come off easily, they are ready. Strain upside-down to drain the water out and serve immediately.

LEMON BUTTER
Melt the butter in a saucepan over medium heat. Add the remaining ingredients and stir until well mixed. Pour into dipping bowls.

- 230 g butter
- ½ cup lemon juice
- ¼ teaspoon salt
- pinch of chilli powder

SERVES 4 AS A STARTER

ASPARAGUS

Bright green asparagus spears popping up are the first sign that spring is on its way. Because I have only a few plants, much of my harvest is eaten right in the garden. Raw asparagus, crisp and crunchy, is the pure taste of spring. However, some does make it to the kitchen and for asparagus the simplest recipes work the best.

Harvesting, buying and storing asparagus

Asparagus needs to develop a strong crown underground before harvesting can begin. If harvested too soon, the plant will be spindly and weak. Resist the temptation for the first couple of years and begin harvesting only in the third year after planting. Harvest when the spears are 15 to 25 cm above the ground. Cut or snap spears off just above the ground. Harvest every 2 to 3 days, for a maximum of 8 weeks. Stop harvesting if the spears become spindly.

When buying asparagus, look for ones with straight, crisp stalks and compact tips. Asparagus does not keep for long and the sooner it is eaten after being picked, the better. If you do have to store it, either wrap the cut ends in a wet paper towel or place them in a shallow bowl of water. Cover with plastic and keep in the salad drawer of the fridge for no longer than 3 days.

Asparagus freezes well, retaining both nutrients and flavour. See page 235 for more on freezing.

Asparagus pesto

Many recipes call for just asparagus tips – this is a great recipe for using up the remaining stalks. The pesto will keep for a couple of weeks in the fridge, as long as the surface is covered with olive oil.

Steam or microwave the asparagus until just tender. In a food processor or using a pestle and mortar, blend the pine nuts, garlic and salt to a coarse purée. Add the olive oil and asparagus, and pulse until the stalks are chopped and the mixture nicely blended. Stir the cheese through using a spoon.

Serve over hot pasta or scoop into a bottle, cover the surface with olive oil and seal.

- 500 g asparagus stalks
- ¼ cup pine nuts
- 3 garlic cloves
- ½ teaspoon salt
- ½ cup extra virgin olive oil
- ¼ cup freshly grated Parmesan cheese

Asparagus and leek on puff pastry

One of my earliest foodie memories is from my grandfather's farm. I was about five, walking with Aunt Margaret, when she spotted wild asparagus growing amongst some rocks. The skinny, green spears did not look like asparagus to me. Asparagus was fat and white and came in tins. But Aunt Margaret knew which wild mushrooms were edible – so if she said this was asparagus, I believed her. We gathered armfuls and later that day I ate my first real asparagus, steamed, with a bowl of lemon butter.

Many years later, in my Johannesburg garden, I picked the first spears I had grown. And I thought about that day and wondered if I would ever have tried growing my own if it hadn't been for Aunt Margaret. This recipe is for her.

Preheat oven to 210°C. Fold the edges of the puff pastry to form a ridge all the way around the rectangle. Brush with melted butter and prick the surface evenly with a fork. Bake for 25 to 30 minutes until golden.

While the pastry is cooking, slice the leeks lengthways, but don't cut all the way through. Place in an ovenproof dish in one layer, fanned open. Drizzle with olive

ASPARAGUS AND LEEK ON PUFF PASTRY

- 1 packet puff pastry
- 2 teaspoons melted butter
- 10 to 15 baby leeks
- olive oil
- salt and pepper to taste
- 10 to 15 asparagus spears, cut into bite-sized pieces
- 4 teaspoons anchovies, chopped
- ½ teaspoon anchovy oil
- 20 baby tomatoes
- 1 tablespoon parsley, chopped
- 1 tablespoon basil, chopped
- ½ teaspoon balsamic vinegar
- 1 teaspoon olive oil
- ¼ cup grated Pecorino
- 1 tablespoon roasted pine nuts

SERVES 4 AS A STARTER

oil and sprinkle with pepper and salt to taste. Place in the oven alongside the puff pastry and cook until softened.

Toss the asparagus with the anchovies and anchovy oil, and set aside. Slice the tomatoes in half and toss with the herbs, balsamic vinegar and olive oil.

When the pastry is cooked, place the leeks in a layer inside the raised edges. Scatter the asparagus and tomatoes over the leeks, and sprinkle the Pecorino cheese and roasted pine nuts on top. Grill for 1 to 2 minutes until the cheese has melted and is browned in places, making sure it doesn't burn.

STEAK

- 4 x 250g fillet steaks
- ½ cup steak rub
  (see page 231)
- olive oil

POTATO WEDGES

- 6 large potatoes, with skins
  on, sliced into wedges
- 2 teaspoons herbal salt
  (see page 53)
- 2 teaspoons Japanese chilli
  (see page 250)
- olive oil

SAUCE

- 1 tablespoon flour
- 1 cup orange juice
- 1 teaspoon Dijon mustard
- ½ tablespoon fresh
  rosemary, finely chopped
- pinch brown sugar
- 1 tablespoon butter

SERVES 4

Fillet steak with potato wedges and asparagus salad

A few years ago I started experimenting with steak rubs – mixing together dried herbs from the garden with various spices and seasonings. One evening, while busy mixing, I accidentally knocked over the coffee container. The smell of the coffee grounds inspired me to add a couple of spoonfuls to my spice rub. That night's steak, with the coffee giving it a rich, baritone bass kick of flavour, was the best I had ever made.

STEAK, POTATO WEDGES AND SAUCE

Rub steaks evenly with steak rub. Leave to stand while you make the potatoes. Once you have popped the potatoes in the oven, prepare the salad.

Heat oven to 210°C. Toss potato wedges in a bowl with the salt, chilli and olive oil until evenly coated. Place in a single layer in a roasting pan and bake for about 40 minutes, turning occasionally, until golden and crispy.

Heat some olive oil in cast iron frying pan until shimmering. Add the steaks and cook, turning once, until cooked to your liking (approximately 3 to 4 minutes per side for medium rare, depending on the thickness of the steak). Remove steaks from the pan, cover and leave to rest while you make the sauce.

Turn the heat to low. Pour off excess oil, leaving only a thin layer. Sprinkle the flour into the steak pan, stirring it into the oil, and cook for 1 to 2 minutes. Slowly add the orange juice, mixing it smoothly with the flour. As it comes to the boil, stir and scrape up any browned bits from the bottom of the pan. Add the Dijon mustard, rosemary and sugar, and stir through until the sauce is smooth. Leave it to simmer and reduce for about 8 minutes, stirring occasionally. Just before serving, stir the butter through the sauce. Taste and add salt if necessary.

ASPARAGUS SALAD

Cut the asparagus into evenly-sized pieces. Heat some olive oil in a pan and sauté asparagus for about 1 to 2 minutes. Add the sesame seeds and stir through. (Black sesame seeds taste the same as white but they add a visual pizzazz to the red and green of this salad.) Add the cherry tomatoes and toss until just heated. Add the balsamic vinegar, sesame oil, sugar, salt and pepper. Stir until blended, remove from heat and leave to cool.

Gently sprinkle the asparagus and tomatoes over the bed of mixed lettuce and greens. Top with the pine nuts.

ASPARAGUS SALAD

- 20 spears fresh asparagus
- olive oil
- 2 tablespoons black sesame seeds
- 20 red cherry tomatoes
- 1 tablespoon fig balsamic vinegar
- 2 tablespoons sesame oil
- pinch sugar
- salt and pepper to taste
- bed of mixed lettuce and greens
- 2 tablespoons pine nuts, toasted

SERVES 4

GARLIC

I only discovered garlic when I was in my mid-twenties. My father didn't like garlic at all so my mother never cooked with it. The upshot was I missed out on garlic for my first twenty years and I had a lot of catching up to do.

Today I adore garlic and can't cook without it. I am not alone. All the robust cuisines that I love – Mexican, Chinese, Thai, Indian and Mediterranean – use garlic extensively. Garlic can be roasted, fried, added to stews, frizzled in oil or eaten raw. As a general rule, for quick-cooking dishes, dice cloves into small evenly-sized pieces and for slow-cooked dishes, use larger pieces. For a useful gadget, which really helps when preparing garlic, see Gadget Girl on page 244.

A delicious way of using garlic is roasting it (see page 227). The resulting rounded and mellow flavour of the roasted version is the complete opposite of the sharpness of fresh garlic and adds wonderful depth to any dish.

Harvesting, buying and storing garlic

Garlic is usually ready from late spring to mid-summer. Once the leaves turn brownish-yellow, check on the heads. There is no need to dig them up, just clear the soil around the top to see how big they are. You want to time it so that the cloves have developed to a decent size, but not so big that the bulbs are beginning to split. When ready, dig them out rather than pulling. Be gentle – fresh garlic bruises easily. They also need to get out of the sun quickly. Dust them off – don't wash them – and plait the tops together. Hang them up in a dark, cool, dry spot for a few weeks until the skin is papery. When shopping for garlic, choose firm, dry heads without any damp or dark spots. If they have green sprouts, leave them.

Whole bulbs will last for months if stored in a dark, well-ventilated place. Once you break the bulb open, its lifetime is reduced, so use the cloves quickly. Don't store in the fridge, as this will make it mouldy. The best way to preserve garlic is to freeze it. This will affect the texture slightly but will retain the taste. Unpeeled cloves can be frozen in sealed containers. Or dice them finely, mix with olive oil and freeze. The oil doesn't freeze solid and you can spoon out what you need.

NOODLES
- oil for deep-frying
- cellophane rice noodles
- I bunch coriander leaves, roughly chopped, for garnishing

FISH
- 750 g firm white fish fillets
- butter

SAUCE
- ¼ cup peanut oil
- 8 spring onions, sliced
- I fresh hot red chilli, sliced
- 4 cloves garlic, diced
- 3 teaspoons grated fresh ginger
- 2 tablespoons light soy sauce
- I tablespoon grated palm sugar
- I teaspoon brown sugar
- I tablespoon tamarind liquid (see page 252)
- I tablespoon fish sauce
- ½ cup orange juice (a 100% unsweetened, blended juice is fine)
- ½ cup water
- ¼ teaspoon freshly ground black pepper

SERVES 4

Thai fish with chilli and coriander

This is one of my earliest recipes, the result of experimenting with Charmaine Solomon's *South East Asian Cooking*. When I first made this dish, a friend said he would eat cardboard if it had this sauce on it. I never put him to the test, but it soon became a firm favourite at dinner parties.

NOODLES
Heat the oil in a medium-sized pot. Cut the noodles into roughly 10 cm lengths, holding them over a bowl so they don't go flying all over the kitchen. Test the oil by dropping in small pieces of noodle. It is hot enough when the noodle immediately puffs up and rises to the surface. Add the cellophane noodles in small batches (they triple in size as they fry). As they puff and rise to the surface, scoop them out with a slotted spoon and drain on paper towels.

FISH
Place the fillets on a baking tray and dot with butter. Cover and bake at 180°C for about 15 to 20 minutes, until cooked through. Remove and break into bite-sized pieces. Cover and keep warm. Make the sauce while the fish is cooking.

SAUCE
Heat the oil in a medium-sized pot until it shimmers. Add the spring onions and stir-fry for about 1 minute, until just softened. Add the chilli, garlic and ginger, and cook over low heat until golden and soft. Add the soy sauce, palm sugar, brown sugar, tamarind liquid, fish sauce, orange juice, water and pepper, and simmer for about 2 minutes.

Serve the fish on a bed of deep-fried cellophane noodles, with sauce spooned over, and top with the fresh coriander leaves. Serve immediately as the noodles start to go soft once the sauce is added.

V Vegetarian option: this spicy yet fresh sauce is a perfect complement to the quiet taste of tofu. Substitute baked or fried tofu for the fish and two teaspoons of marmite for the fish sauce.

- 500 g calamari rings
- juice of a lime
- 2 garlic cloves, diced
- 1 tablespoon lemon grass
- 1 red chilli, sliced into rings
- 2 tablespoons peanut oil
- 1 teaspoon red Thai curry paste
- 1/4 teaspoon sugar
- 1 x 400 ml tin coconut milk
- salt to taste
- fresh coriander

SERVES 4 AS A STARTER

'In Food we trust' calamari curry

On the way back from a video shoot in Dubai we flew via the Comoros. On the spur of the moment, Keith and I hopped off the plane and stayed for a few days. Near the beach was a small restaurant with about four tables, run by Madame Marie. Her food was so good we ate there three nights in a row.

On our last night she asked us if we could please do her a favour. Could we take some money to her son who was studying in Johannesburg? We agreed and she entrusted two strangers, who had relished her food, with R2 000 to take to her son. All she knew about us was our first names and that we loved her food.

This fresh, light curry is for Madame Marie – and all others like her. In Food we trust.

Mix the calamari with the lime juice, garlic, chopped lemon grass and chilli. Marinate for 2 to 3 hours.

Heat the peanut oil in a wok over high heat until it shimmers. Add the calamari with the marinade to the wok. Cook, stirring, for 2 to 3 minutes. Pour off the liquid and reserve. Stir-fry the calamari over high heat for a further 4 to 5 minutes, adding more oil if necessary. Add the curry paste and stir until the calamari is well coated. Add the reserved marinade, sugar and the coconut milk and stir through. Simmer gently for 2 to 3 minutes until thickened slightly. Add salt to taste.

Sprinkle generously with coriander and serve with jasmine rice. This curry is quite liquid. Serve the rice in separate bowls and eat using the method described on page 76. The distinctive flavour of fresh coriander defines this delicious curry.

V Vegetarian option: replace the calamari with slices of eggplant. Salt them and leave to stand for half an hour. Rinse well and drain. Continue as per the recipe above, but only marinate them for an hour.

Deep-fried garlic

One of my favourite additions to many a meal is a topping of deep-fried garlic. This is available from any Chinese supermarket but you can easily make your own. Golden, deep-fried garlic adds a wonderful crunchy flavour to stir-fries and noodle soups. The oil becomes infused with the garlic and adds great depth to dishes.

- ½ cup olive oil
- 4 tablespoons diced garlic cloves

Heat the oil in a pan until shimmering. Test the oil temperature by dropping one piece of garlic into the pan and if it sizzles, the oil is ready. Add the garlic and stir to separate, so that it cooks evenly. Cook, stirring occasionally, for a minute or so until half the garlic has changed to a caramel colour. Remove from the heat and strain the garlic out of the oil. Leave both to cool. Store the oil separately from the garlic in sterilised bottles (see page 239). Seal and keep in the fridge for up to a week. (To make deep-fried onion sprinkles, follow the recipe above, substituting finely chopped onion for the garlic.)

ONIONS

The aroma of onions spreading through the house, whether slowly sweetening in olive oil or stir-frying with a sizzle, is enough for Keith to call out 'Mmmm, that smells delicious – what are you cooking?'

I don't like raw onions and I will always adapt a recipe to make sure that the onions are well cooked, as for example in the kofta recipe on page 32. Most meatball or kofta recipes mix raw onion with the meat, but I like to cook it first to take off the raw edge. Another way of softening the taste of raw onions is to mix them with an acidic ingredient. This works particularly well with sweet red onions. Before using them in a salad, mix them with balsamic vinegar and some herbs and leave to stand for an hour or so.

Onions can be slowly cooked until they caramelise, quickly sautéed until crisp, or roasted whole for melt-in-the-mouth flavour. Whichever way you cook them, you have to prepare them first.

Onion fact: they make you cry. As soon as you slice into an onion cell, enzymes are released that form a gas that makes your eyes tear. There are many old wives' tales of how to prevent this but I haven't found any that work. The only way is to reduce the effect by using as sharp a knife as possible, and to keep tissues handy. A good onion cry can be very cleansing! For more on preparing onions see page 238.

Harvesting, buying and storing onions

Harvest onions when the base has swelled up and the leaves are yellowy brown. Leave them in the sun for a day or so, then move them to a well-ventilated, shady spot for a few weeks to dry. They are ready to store when the skins are papery and the roots wiry. Once dry, cut the tops off, leaving 8 cm of leaves.

When buying onions, look for ones that are heavy for their size and have papery skins without any damp or discoloured patches. They store best in a dark spot with good ventilation. A basket or a brown paper bag is a good idea. Moisture will rot onions quickly; so keep them out of fridges and plastic bags.

Lamb kofta in a chickpea, spinach and tomato sauce

The Turkish name 'kofta' is far more romantic than English 'meatballs'. The fresh seasonal herbs mixed into the meat make all the difference to this dish. The meat mixture can also be made into longer sausage shapes, threaded onto a skewer and cooked over a fire.

KOFTA

- olive oil
- 1 large onion, finely chopped
- 500 g minced lamb
- 2 cloves garlic, diced
- 1/8 teaspoon ground cloves
- 1/4 teaspoon ground nutmeg
- 1/4 teaspoon hot paprika
- 1/2 teaspoon ground cumin
- 1/2 teaspoon ground coriander
- 1 teaspoon finely chopped lemon zest
- 1/4 cup pine nuts, chopped
- 1/4 cup fresh parsley, chopped
- 1/4 cup fresh mint, chopped
- 1/2 cup bread crumbs
- 1 egg, beaten
- salt and pepper to taste

SERVES 4

KOFTA

Heat the oil in a small pan and cook the onion over medium heat for about 5 to 8 minutes, stirring occasionally, until soft. While the onion is cooking, mix the lamb with all the other ingredients in a large bowl. When the onion is ready, add it to the meat and mix it in well. Refrigerate for 30 minutes.

Shape into balls and place on an oiled baking tray. Grill until browned, then turn the kofta and grill until the other side is browned. Serve with a chickpea, spinach and tomato sauce and some pita bread on the side.

CHICKPEA, SPINACH AND TOMATO SAUCE

Heat the oil in a medium-sized pot and cook the onion over medium heat, stirring occasionally, until soft. Add the garlic and cook gently until soft. Add all the spices and stir until the mixture is fragrant and sticky. Then add the chickpeas, tomatoes, dates and water. Bring to the boil, then reduce heat and simmer for 6 to 10 minutes. Finally, add the spinach and stir through until wilted.

Just before serving, stir in the mint, coriander and salt and pepper to taste. The fresh herbs accentuate the flavours of this delicious, fragrant sauce.

V Vegetarian option: the chickpea, spinach and tomato sauce is delicious with falafel.

CHICKPEA, SPINACH AND TOMATO SAUCE

- 2 tablespoons olive oil
- 1 medium onion, finely chopped
- 3 cloves garlic, chopped
- 1 teaspoon ground cinnamon
- 1 teaspoon ground sweet paprika
- 2 teaspoons ground coriander
- 2 teaspoons cumin seeds, roasted
- 2 x 400 g cans chickpeas, drained and rinsed
- 410 g bottled tomatoes (see page 225)
- ¼ cup seedless dates, chopped
- ½ cup water
- 1 bunch spinach, washed and roughly chopped
- 2 tablespoons mint, chopped
- ¼ cup coriander leaves, roughly chopped
- salt and pepper to taste

SERVES 4

- 2 tablespoons olive oil
- 50 g butter
- 5 onions (white or red), sliced
- 2 tablespoons brown sugar
- pinch of salt
- 1 cup medium dry sherry
- 3 tablespoons balsamic vinegar

Onion marmalade

I go through bottles of this because I eat it with everything. It is delicious paired with creamy Camembert or rich Gorgonzola, or dolloped on top of hamburgers, or with ham and avocado on top of crisp bruschetta. Once you start using it – you won't stop!

Heat the olive oil and butter in a heavy-bottomed pan. Add the onion and cook over low heat for about 15 minutes, stirring occasionally, until soft and translucent. Add the brown sugar, salt, sherry and balsamic vinegar and stir until sugar has dissolved.

Simmer for a further 15 to 20 minutes, stirring occasionally until the sauce has thickened and is sticky. Spoon into sterilised bottles (see page 239) and seal.

For a spicy alternative, cook dried chilli flakes, black mustard, cumin and coriander seeds in the butter and oil for a few minutes before adding the onions.

Portuguese fish coconut curry

I am allergic to shellfish, hence there are no shellfish recipes in this book! Nuno, the owner of a popular Melville restaurant, happily makes a fish curry for me instead of the prawn one on his menu. This recipe is inspired by his delicious one.

Heat olive oil in a large heavy-bottomed pot and add the onion. Cook over medium heat, stirring occasionally, for 5 to 8 minutes until starting to turn brown. Add the garlic and cook for 1 to 2 minutes until it softens. Add the chilli and ginger, and cook for a further 2 minutes. Then add the spices, stirring until fragrant and sticky.

Add the coconut cream and simmer until slightly thickened. Add the tomatoes and coconut milk and bring to a simmer. Then add the lime juice, sugar and vegetables, and simmer for 5 to 8 minutes more. Finally, add the fish and stir through gently. Simmer until just cooked, for about another 5 to 6 minutes. Serve over basmati rice sprinkled with fresh coriander leaves.

PORTUGUESE FISH COCONUT CURRY

- 2 tablespoons olive oil
- 1 large onion, sliced
- 5 cloves garlic, diced
- 2 fresh red chillies, sliced
- 1 teaspoon ginger, finely chopped
- 1 tablespoon black mustard seeds
- 1 tablespoon garam masala
- 1 tablespoon coriander
- 1 tablespoon cumin
- 1 teaspoon salt
- 1 x 400 ml can coconut cream
- 1 x 410 g bottled tomatoes (see page 225)
- 1 x 400 ml can coconut milk
- juice of half a lime
- 2 teaspoons grated palm sugar
- 150 g baby carrots, thinly sliced
- 100 g fresh green beans, cut into bite-sized pieces
- 750 g firm white fish, cut into bite-sized pieces
- fresh coriander leaves

SERVES 4

V Vegetarian option: increase the amount of carrots and beans and replace the fish with 2 or 3 potatoes, cooked and cut into bite-sized pieces.

PLUMS

I have chosen to feature plums for spring because the plum tree in my garden is over one hundred years old. Despite its age, it bears phenomenal quantities of fruit and every year I experiment with new plum recipes. I have made plum jam, plum jelly, plum butter, plum cordial, plum chutney and more. I owe it to this elder of my garden to harvest the abundance she gives. If you have other fruit trees in your garden, you can easily adapt the following recipes.

Harvesting, buying and storing plums

Plums ripen over a period of 2 to 3 weeks. During this time, I harvest every day. For cooking I pick up the ones on the ground, discarding any that are already rotten, but keeping those that are bird-nibbled. There is still plenty of fruit on them and they get a good wash before cooking. For eating I pick the most luscious ones with no marks. When buying plums, use your nose – ripe plums smell like plums. Choose ones that are heavy for their size. Slightly unripe plums will continue to ripen indoors. Ripe plums will keep for a week or so in the fridge.

Plum 'starter' recipe

For years I spent ages cutting up plums and taking out the pips. In the process I would lose a lot of the flesh, and I would end up with cuts all over my fingers from the sharp plum stones. There had to be another way. After experimenting I have come up with a much quicker method. This recipe is the base for all my plum jams, jellies and cordials. It can be adapted to many different types of fruit, especially those with large pips.

Collect a large colander of plums and dump them into a basin of water. Wash them well, rubbing or cutting off any bits that have gone bad. Put the washed fruit in a large pot and add enough water so that the level is just below the top of the plums. Bring to the boil and cook for about 8 minutes. For fruit with firmer flesh, such as peaches, increase the amount of cooking time. Turn the heat off, cover and leave for 20 minutes.

At this point you have a choice. If you are making jelly or cordial, pour the plums and liquid into a bowl lined with mutton cloth. Gather the edges and secure them with a strong rubber band. Tie the resulting 'bag' above the bowl and leave to drip overnight. Don't squeeze or disturb the bag as this will result in a cloudy liquid.

If you are making jam or chutney, pour the cooked plums into a colander and, using a potato masher or wooden spoon, push the plum pulp through the holes, until just the pips are left behind.

The strained plum liquid or the plum pulp can be frozen in zip lock bags for later use. This takes the pressure off having to cook the entire harvest as it ripens.

Rose petal plum jelly

The subtle lavender and rose flavours underscore this tart yet sweet jelly. It is delicious with creamy Brie or Camembert. It is also scrumptious dolloped over plain yoghurt. If you want to try making some other flavoured jellies, vanilla and mint both work well.

Mix the plum liquid and the sugar in a large pot, stirring occasionally over low heat until dissolved. Add the lavender sprigs and turn up the heat. Boil, stirring occasionally, until the mixture reaches gelling point (see page 240). Remove from the heat and add the port and rose water.

   Pour into sterilised bottles (see page 239) and top each with a rose petal. Use a skewer to push the rose petal under the surface of the jelly and seal.

   Note: don't be tempted to double this recipe if you have large quantities of fruit. Rather cook it in batches using these proportions. If you increase them, it takes a lot longer to reach gelling point.

- 6 cups of strained plum liquid (see recipe for plum starter on page 38)
- 6 cups sugar
- 6 lavender sprigs
- 3 tablespoons port
- 2 teaspoons rose water
- 12 to 15 rose petals

Plum cordial with lemon verbena

When I was writing my first book I spent many months communicating with Ceri, my publisher, via email before we finally met. It was a hot summer's day and within a few minutes of arriving in my kitchen, she was cooling off with a tall glass of plum cordial. She still talks about it. Ceri, this recipe is for you.

Mix the plum liquid and the sugar together in a large pot over medium heat, stirring to dissolve the sugar. Add the lemon verbena leaves and bring to the boil, cooking for 5 minutes. Discard the lemon verbena leaves and pour the cordial into sterilised bottles (see page 239) and seal. Once opened, keep in the fridge.

   For a deliciously different taste, try substituting rose geranium or mint for the lemon verbena. To serve, mix the cordial in a ratio of about 7 parts sparkling or soda water to 1 part cordial and add a squeeze of lime juice. Top with a lemon verbena leaf.

- 2 cups strained plum liquid (see page 38)
- 1½ cups sugar
- 10 lemon verbena leaves

Crispy pork with Chinese plum sauce

This was the first recipe of mine to be published. A journalist from the *Sunday Times* came to Melville's Bamboo market (held on the first Saturday of every month) where I was selling rose petal plum jelly (page 41) and herbal salt (page 53). We started chatting and a week later she was in my garden, interviewing me under the century-old plum tree. She asked if I could come up with a plum recipe for her readers – and here it is. This recipe makes enough to serve with the pork plus some extra for bottling.

CHINESE PLUM SAUCE

In a heavy-bottomed pot, cook the onions in olive oil until soft, stirring occasionally. Add the ginger and garlic and cook for a further 2 to 3 minutes. Add the plum pulp and all remaining ingredients, except for the chocolate and salt. Bring to the boil and then reduce to a simmer.

Simmer for 15 to 20 minutes, stirring occasionally, until the sauce has thickened. Add the chocolate, stirring through as it melts. Add some salt to taste. Remove from the heat and pour into sterilised bottles (see page 239) and seal, or use with pork.

PORK

To make the pork, place the cornflour and salt in a plastic bag. Add the pork chunks and toss until coated. Heat the oil in a wok and fry the pork in batches until crisp. Keep warm until all the pork is cooked. Serve on a bed of jasmine rice, drizzled with plum sauce and topped with spring onions, carrots and coriander.

V Vegetarian option: instead of pork, use firm tofu.

CHINESE PLUM SAUCE

- 2 onions, finely sliced
- olive oil
- 2 teaspoons finely chopped fresh ginger
- 3 cloves garlic, chopped
- 2 ½ cups plum pulp (see recipe on page 38)
- 1 cup brown sugar
- ¼ cup rice vinegar
- 2 teaspoons dried coriander
- 1 tablespoon dark soy sauce
- pinch ground cinnamon
- ½ teaspoon chilli powder
- pinch ground cloves
- ¼ teaspoon Chinese 5 spice powder
- ¼ cup sweet chilli sauce
- 2 squares dark chocolate
- salt to taste

PORK

- 2 tablespoons cornflour
- 1 teaspoon salt
- 1 pork fillet, cut into small chunks
- oil for frying
- 6 spring onions, chopped
- 2 large carrots, finely slivered
- fresh coriander leaves

SERVES 2

Spring Herbs

Even if there is nothing else growing, I will always have some fresh herbs in the garden and I use them year round in my kitchen. The simplest meal becomes sublime just by adding fresh basil, chives, coriander or parsley.

I also keep a collection of dried herbs in my pantry as certain recipes respond better to dried than fresh herbs. By late spring, many herbs, especially the Mediterranean ones, are at their best. The summer heat hasn't dried them out yet and they are full of succulent leaves, before starting to set flowers. This is the perfect time to preserve them.

Harvesting, buying and storing herbs

Many herbs are perennial and most are easy as pie to grow. Even if you don't have a vegetable garden, they are simple to grow in pots on a windowsill. Pick herbs early in the morning before the day's heat begins to wilt them. Don't just trim the tops, rather cut a branch or stem back by at least two thirds. This will encourage the plant to grow more leaves. To strip fresh leaves off herbs with woody stems, like rosemary and thyme, hold the tip of the stem firmly and pull the leaves off, from the tip backwards.

When buying, avoid herbs with black or brown marks on them. Look for ones that are sprightly and fresh, not limp and dull.

Some herbs dry better than others. Mediterranean herbs (rosemary, lavender, oregano, marjoram and thyme) retain their flavour well when dried. To dry Mediterranean herbs, leave them on the stem. Tie the stems together with string and hang them in a cool, dry spot until the leaves are crisp. Pull the leaves off using the same method as for fresh ones, and store in airtight bottles. Softer leafed herbs, such as dill, fennel, parsley and basil don't keep their flavour for as long when dried. Dry these herbs by removing the leaves from the stems and spreading them evenly on a paper towel on a rack. Place in the sun until the leaves are papery. Herbs not suited for drying are coriander and chives.

Avocado and watercress salad with herbal salt roast vegetables

ROAST VEGETABLES

- 2 potatoes
- 1 sweet potato
- 4 carrots
- 2 onions
- 1 small butternut
- olive oil
- herbal salt to taste
  (see page 53)
- fresh coriander or parsley

SALAD

- 2 tablespoons sesame oil
- 3 tablespoons rice vinegar
- 1½ tablespoons sushi
  soy sauce
- 2 tablespoons mirin
- ½ teaspoon brown sugar
- ½ apple, grated
- 1 bowl of fresh watercress,
  washed and spun-dried
- 2 large avocado pears,
  chopped into chunks
- ½ cup pecan nuts, roughly
  chopped

SERVES 4

Watercress is a herb that is at its best in spring. It is also very good for us, containing loads of vitamin C and minerals.

I love the simplicity of this salad, with the grated apple adding a surprise touch. Its freshness complements the heartiness of the roast vegetables. (If you don't have watercress in your garden, substitute rocket.) The secret to roasting vegetables successfully is to spread them out on a large baking tray, evenly spaced and not resting on top of one another. For that yummy caramelised roasted flavour to develop, they need space around them for the hot air to circulate.

ROAST VEGETABLES

Preheat the oven to 200° C. Scrub the potatoes, sweet potato and carrots and dry them well. Peel the onions and butternut. Scoop out the butternut seeds and discard. Cut the vegetables into evenly-sized pieces. Toss with olive oil and herbal salt and spread out onto a baking tray. (Use 2 if necessary.)

Bake for 20 minutes and then toss the vegetables to prevent them from sticking, spreading them evenly in the baking tray. Bake for further 20 to 40 minutes, depending on the size of the vegetable chunks, until cooked through. Top with fresh coriander or parsley just before serving.

SALAD

Mix the first 6 ingredients together, whisking well until the sugar has dissolved. Toss the dressing with the watercress and place in a serving bowl. Add the avocado pear and toss gently. Sprinkle with the pecan nuts and serve with the roasted vegetables.

DIPPING SAUCE

- ¼ cup water
- ½ cup fresh lime juice
- ½ cup finely grated palm sugar
- ⅓ cup fish sauce
- 1 tablespoon chopped fresh coriander
- 2 fresh small red chillies, chopped finely
- ¼ cup crushed peanuts

Vietnamese rice paper wraps

These refreshing and delicious rolls are much easier to make than traditional deep-fried spring rolls – and more unusual.

The balance between the fresh ingredients and the spicy sweet dipping sauce is superb. Play around with different fillings to suit your pantry and taste.

It is best to have all the filling ingredients ready and waiting, before starting to wrap the rolls. And, instead of going through the hassle of rolling them all yourself, have dinner guests roll their own. It is lots of fun and makes for a very sociable meal.

DIPPING SAUCE

Mix all the ingredients together, stirring until the sugar has dissolved. Divide amongst 6 dipping bowls. The flavour of this sauce improves if it is left to sit for a couple of hours before serving.

RICE PAPER WRAPS

Heat the peanut oil in a wok until shimmering. Add the chicken and stir-fry until cooked. Add salt and chilli to taste. Remove from heat and cool.

Bring a pot of water to a rolling boil over high heat. Add the rice vermicelli and remove from heat. Leave to stand for about 8 minutes, stirring the noodles occasionally so they don't clump together. Drain in a colander and rinse with cold water.

Tear the mint, coriander and basil leaves into small pieces and mix together in one bowl. Prepare the vegetables and have them standing ready in separate bowls. Place a bowl of warm water and a damp kitchen towel on the work surface. Working with one piece of rice paper at a time, dip it into the warm water for about 30 seconds to soften. Turn it so that it softens evenly. Put it on the damp kitchen towel, to prevent it from sticking to the work surface.

Place a layer of filling along one side of the rice paper, starting with noodles and chicken, and topping with the vegetables and herbs. Leave a bit of space at the sides so that you can seal the roll. Don't make the filling too fat otherwise the parcel will be difficult to roll. Roll the rice paper to form a sausage, enclosing the filling. (You don't want to roll so tightly that it tears, but you also need to roll it firmly so it holds the filling. You will get the hang of it after the first one or two.) When you reach half way, fold the side edges in, enclosing the filling.

Place on a tray, seam side down, covered with a damp dishtowel, until you are ready to serve. Just before serving, slice each wrap in half.

If guests are rolling their own, supply extra damp towels and bowls of warm water for dipping and rolling the rice paper.

V Vegetarian option: replace the chicken with slices of avocado pear. Strips of grilled haloumi cheese also taste good.

RICE PAPER WRAPS

- 1½ tablespoons peanut oil
- 200 g chicken breast, sliced into strips
- salt and Japanese chilli to taste
- 100 g rice vermicelli
- ½ cup fresh Vietnamese mint leaves (or ordinary mint)
- ½ cup fresh coriander leaves
- ½ cup fresh basil leaves
- 1 cup finely sliced green and red baby cabbage
- ½ cup bean sprouts
- ½ cup matchstick-size strips seeded cucumber
- ½ cup matchstick-size strips peeled carrot
- 12 round rice paper sheets (plus a few extra in case any break)

MAKES 24

FISH

- 125 g flour
- 3 teaspoons cornflour
- 1 teaspoon baking powder
- ½ teaspoon salt
- 1 egg
- 235 ml beer
- 500 g hake fillets, cut into bite-sized pieces
- flour for dusting
- oil for deep-frying

CABBAGE AND SAUCE

- 120 ml plain yoghurt
- 120 ml mayonnaise
- juice of a lime
- 1 jalapeno pepper, finely chopped
- pinch of salt
- 1 teaspoon freshly chopped dill
- ½ teaspoon ground cayenne pepper
- ½ baby red cabbage
- ½ baby green cabbage

TO SERVE

- 12 corn tacos
- lime wedges
- fresh dill

SERVES 6

Fish tacos with crunchy cabbage and tangy sauce

I ate these in Arizona, washed down with a chilli beer – jalapeno-flavoured beer, which is surprisingly delicious! Crunchy, tangy and tasty, fish tacos are perfect to serve on a hot spring day, especially at the beach. Make extra because they are very moreish.

Fresh dill is the perfect herb to complement fish dishes and works particularly well with this taco filling. Cabbages can grow almost all year round and baby cabbages are particularly delicious in spring.

Oh – and if you want to serve the chilli beer, simply pierce a whole pickled jalapeno a few times with a toothpick. Pop it into a beer mug and add the beer. Leave it in the fridge for a few minutes before serving.

FISH

Combine the flour, cornflour, baking powder and salt in a large bowl. In a jug, beat the egg with a fork until smooth and add the beer, stirring well. Pour the egg and beer mixture into the flour, stirring quickly. Don't worry if there are a few lumps. Leave to stand while you prepare the cabbage and sauce.

To fry the fish, heat oil to 190° C. Using tongs, dip the fish pieces into some flour and then into the beer batter. Drop into the oil and deep-fry until crisp and golden brown. Drain on paper towels and keep warm while you cook the rest.

CABBAGE AND SAUCE

In a medium-sized bowl, mix the yoghurt, mayonnaise and lime juice together until smooth. Add the next four ingredients and mix well. Transfer the sauce to a serving bowl. Toss the finely sliced cabbage together in a separate serving bowl.

TO SERVE

Place a few pieces of fried fish in the bottom of a taco shell and squeeze over a little lime juice. Top with shredded cabbage, drizzle with some tangy sauce and finish off with lots of fresh dill leaves.

V Vegetarian option: substitute deep-fried tofu for the fish.

- 2 slices of bread
- butter, softened
- Cajun or Curry spice mix (see page 229 and 231)
- 2 large eggs
- salt and pepper to taste
- 1 teaspoon chopped chives

SERVES 2

Eggs in a hole

My mother is an extremely creative and inventive cook. My school lunch boxes were legendary. Come break times, I would unpack a complicated arrangement of lovingly prepared food. Even my sandwiches were not straightforward – they were layered delights called 'Rainbow sandwiches'. This egg recipe is one that Mom would make often and is a perfect example of how she would take something as ordinary as egg and bread and give it her special Mom twist.

Butter both sides of the bread. Sprinkle liberally with the spice mix and use the butter knife to mix it into the butter. Cut a square out of the middle of each slice of bread. Place the two slices and the cut-outs in a pan and cook over medium heat until one side is browned. Turn all pieces over and add a small pat of butter to the hole in the middle of each slice of bread. Carefully break an egg into the centre of each hole. Season with salt and pepper to taste, and sprinkle the chives onto the egg yolks. Cover the pan with a lid. Cook until the eggs are just set and serve straightaway. Yummy for a brunch.

Herbal salt

This method of storing herbs' fresh spring flavour uses a natural preservative: salt. Herbal salt is a staple in my kitchen. I find it particularly tasty with roast vegetables or chicken. It can be added during the cooking process, where the herb flavour will permeate the food, or it can be sprinkled on afterwards to add a herbal zing to the finished dish. It is also delicious with any egg dishes. And fish too. In fact, use it wherever you would usually use ordinary salt!

Gather a colander of mixed herbs such as marjoram, oregano, rosemary, winter savoury and thyme. Wash and dry them well, using a salad spinner then dishcloths. Strip off the leaves, discarding any woody stems. Using a food processor, chop the herbs in stages until fine.

Measure the herbs and for every cup of herbs, add two cups of sea salt and half a teaspoon of lime or lemon zest. Mix together well. Using a blender, finely blend one cup of the mixture at a time until the salt is smooth and pale green. Store in airtight bottles.

Three cheese quesadillas with spinach

Quesadillas (pronounced *kess a diyas*) mean 'little cheeses' in Spanish. These tortilla 'sandwiches' are a popular Mexican street food, served with a variety of fillings. They are one of my favourite quick meals, and kids love them too. Many other fillings can be used – just follow the basic procedure and experiment with what you have handy. This is a great way to use up leftovers.

- 20 to 30 large spinach leaves, washed and spun dry
- olive oil
- 2 cloves garlic, diced
- 1 tablespoon butter
- pepper and salt to taste
- 8 flour tortillas
- 1 x 410 g Mexican flavoured tomatoes (see page 226)
- ½ cup feta cheese, cubed
- ½ cup mozzarella cheese, cubed
- ½ cup cheddar cheese, grated
- chopped chives
- fresh coriander leaves

SERVES 4

Cut out centre stalks of the spinach and slice them finely. Roughly chop the leaves. Heat the oil in a pan over medium heat. Add the garlic and sauté for a minute. Add the chopped stems and sauté for a further minute. Add the chopped leaves and sauté for 2 minutes more. Add the butter, pepper and salt. Stir together for about a minute and remove from the heat.

Spread 4 tortillas with a layer of Mexican tomato. Add a layer of cooked spinach. Scatter the feta, mozzarella and cheddar over the top. Cover each one with a second tortilla, pressing down so the filling is flattened slightly.

Heat a pan over medium heat (I use the same one I cooked the spinach in, wiped with a paper towel). Place the first quesadilla in the centre of the pan, making sure no filling falls out. Cook for about 3 to 4 minutes, gently pressing the top down with a spatula. To turn it over, invert a plate over the top of the quesadilla. Holding the plate firmly in place with one hand, turn the entire frying pan over so the quesadilla falls onto the plate. Do it quickly so it flips and doesn't slide. (If you are feeling adventurous, you can try and flip it like a pancake – but be warned, it can be messy!)

Put the frying pan back on the heat and using a spatula, slide the quesadilla from the plate back into the frying pan and cook the other side for 2 to 3 minutes, pressing down gently until cooked. Keep it warm while you cook the others. Serve sprinkled with fresh chives and coriander.

STRAWBERRIES

If you don't grow your own strawberries try to find a strawberry-picking farm near you. From mid-September to mid-December, depending on the weather, many farmers open their strawberry fields to the public. You can either pay an entrance fee and eat as much as you like, or take a basket home.

An organically grown, sun-ripened strawberry is so far removed from the sad specimens you find on many supermarket shelves. Buying a bright red strawberry and biting into it to find that it tastes of … nothing, is enough to make my taste buds go on strike.

Harvesting, buying and storing strawberries

Harvest strawberries when they are firm and red – about a month after they start flowering. Pick early in the morning before the day heats up. They are best eaten within a day or two of being picked. Wash them just before using – they will last longer in the fridge unwashed.

When buying strawberries, don't make the mistake of thinking bigger is better – the smaller ones often taste sweeter. Look for firm red ones, without any blemishes.

Strawberries, as with all berries, can easily be frozen whole (see page 235). Although the texture will be a bit mushy if allowed to defrost completely, they retain their flavour. Frozen strawberries are best used in baking or blended to make smoothies or ice cream. If you have excess strawberries, make preserves or jam (see page 60).

- 200 g caster sugar
  (plus another 150 g)
- ¼ cup water
- ½ cup slivered almonds
- zest of a lemon
- 2 cups strawberries, washed
  and hulled
- ¼ cup water (or less)
- 500 ml cream
- 4 eggs
- 1 teaspoon vanilla essence
- extra strawberries for
  decoration

SERVES 16

Strawberry and almond semifreddo

Whether ice cream was invented in Naples or not is a moot point. But it is an undisputed fact that in Naples they make the most delicious ice cream I have ever tasted. The secret? They use all natural products and the freshest ingredients. We took a trip to Naples recently, and just near our hotel there was a *gelateria* – so every day we would devour scoops of strawberry, pistachio or caramel delight.

Back home I wanted to try and make my own, but as I don't have an ice cream maker, I explored recipes that don't need one. *Semifreddo* literally means 'semi-frozen' and its fluffiness comes from the whipped egg whites and cream.

For a delicious variation, try making a triple lemon flavoured version instead of strawberry. When making the syrup, add a handful of lemon verbena leaves and a couple of bruised lemon grass stalks. Before pouring out the syrup, strain it, and then add the lemon zest.

Have 2 one-litre containers standing by. (You can use plastic ice cream ones, or pretty moulds if it is for a dinner party.) Stir 200 g caster sugar and the water together in a small pot over medium heat until the sugar has melted. Bring to a boil and add the slivered almonds. Reduce the heat and simmer for about 5 minutes, then add the lemon zest and remove from the heat. Pour the mixture onto a flat tray or plate and spread it out evenly. When it is completely cool, it will have crystallised. Using a pastry scraper or your hands, break it into crumbly pieces.

Whiz the strawberries in a blender, adding sufficient water until they are thick and smooth, and set aside. Pour the cream into a medium-sized bowl and whip until thick.

Separate the eggs, placing the yolks in a medium-sized bowl and the whites in a large one. Beat the yolks together with the remaining 150 g caster sugar and the vanilla essence until creamy. Beat the egg whites until stiff. Fold the egg yolk and sugar mixture into the egg whites and stir very gently until well mixed.

Add the whipped cream to the egg mixture and stir until mixed through. Scrape the sugared almonds and zest mixture from the tray into the bowl, leaving enough

to decorate the top of the semifreddo, and stir it in. Pour a layer of the mixture into each one-litre container. Add a drizzle of the blended strawberries and swirl it through the mixture. You don't want to over-mix it; you want to create streaks of pinky-red. Repeat layering and adding the strawberries until it is all in the containers. Sprinkle the rest of the sugared almonds over the top and freeze for 3 to 4 hours before serving. Top with sliced, fresh strawberries.

Strawberry jam

The first time I visited a strawberry-picking farm I was so carried away by the abundance of berries that I picked far more than we could possibly eat. Faced with these bulging baskets, I had to make jam. Now, whenever I go, I pick more than I need, just so I can make jam.

There is nothing quite as welcoming as freshly baked scones topped with homemade strawberry jam and a dollop of cream. For a delicious alternative, add a couple of sprigs of lavender or mint when you bring the mixture to the boil. Remove the herbs before bottling the jam.

- 4 cups ripe strawberries, stalks removed and halved
- 2 cups sugar
- ¼ cup lemon juice

Mix the berries and the sugar in a bowl, cover and leave to stand for a few hours, mushing them up occasionally to break the strawberries into pieces.

Tip the strawberry mixture and lemon juice into a pot and bring to the boil slowly, stirring. Keep at a rolling boil, stirring occasionally, until the jam reaches the 'wrinkle' stage (see page 240) or 105°C. Ladle into sterilised jars and seal (see page 239).

Strawberry, avocado and radish salad with balsamic dressing

Whoever first paired strawberries with balsamic is a gourmet genius. The sour-sweet taste of the vinegar makes strawberries become, well, more strawberry! Combine sweet red strawberries, piquant white radishes and creamy green avocado for a deliciously fresh salad that is not just about the fusion of tastes; but also about the visually tantalising play of colours.

- large bowl mixed lettuce leaves
- 20 strawberries, cut in half
- 10 radishes, thinly sliced
- 1 avocado pear, cut into chunks
- 3 tablespoons olive oil
- 1 tablespoon balsamic reduction
- salt and freshly ground black pepper

SERVES 4

Arrange the lettuce on a serving platter. Mix the strawberries and radishes together, taking care not to crush the berries, and toss over the leaves. Toss the avocado chunks lightly into the salad.

Whisk the olive oil and balsamic vinegar together, and add salt and pepper to taste. (I recommend the delicious locally made balsamic reduction, Black Gold.) Drizzle the dressing over the salad and serve.

Boston Tea Party strawberry and lemon cheesecake

I made my first ever cheesecake when we stayed in Boston with Keith's cousin Ed. It was for his birthday tea party, so of course it had to be the Boston Tea Party cheesecake. It is best prepared the day before, with just the strawberry topping made on the day. I use Philadelphia cream cheese for this recipe — it's expensive, but it makes the best cheesecake!

CRUST

Process the biscuits until roughly chopped. Add the butter and zest and mix until well combined. Using a straight-sided glass, press the mixture evenly into the base and up the sides of a 20 cm springform cake tin. Refrigerate for an hour.

FILLING

Heat the oven to 180°C. Beat the eggs and caster sugar until thick and creamy. Add the cream cheese, lemon zest and juice, blending until smooth. Pour into the biscuit base and bake for an hour. Cool, then refrigerate overnight.

TOPPING

Melt the strawberry jam, liqueur and verjuice together in a pan over medium heat until well mixed and runny. Leave to cool slightly. Remove the cheesecake from the springform pan carefully. Top with a spiral of strawberry halves. Spoon the jam mixture evenly over the top and refrigerate for an hour.

CRUST

- 2 ½ cups biscuits (200 g Marie or Tennis)
- 160 g melted butter
- 2 tablespoons lemon zest, finely chopped

FILLING

- 2 eggs
- ¾ cup caster sugar
- 2 × 250 g Philadelphia cream cheese (room temperature)
- 1 tablespoon lemon zest
- ¼ cup lemon juice

TOPPING

- 1 cup strawberry jam
- 3 tablespoons Grand Marnier liqueur
- 3 tablespoons verjuice
- 2 cups strawberries, halved

SERVES 8 TO 10

DECEMBER 22 – MARCH 21

Dirty hands, iced tea, garden fragrances thick in the air and a blanket of colour before me, who could ask for more?
Bev Adams

By mid-December the vegetable garden is producing at full throttle and it breaks my heart to go away for Christmas. The slender green beans, the bunches of tomatoes that have only just begun to ripen, the baby marrows and squash will all be at their best while I am away. Well, that's the way I feel when I say goodbye. However, I'm always proved wrong. As long as they are looked after and harvested regularly, these summer vegetables will continue producing for months.

IN SEASON IN SUMMER

Basil	Eggplant	Spring onions
Beans	Lemon verbena	Summer squash
Beetroot	Lemon grass	Sweet corn
Carrots	Mint	Swiss chard
Chillies	Peppers	Tomatoes
Cucumber	Rosemary	

SUMMER

BASIL

I grow as many different kinds of basil as I can squeeze into my space. From the bright green, large-leafed Genovese basil to the pointed-leafed, darker green Siam Queen, they are all used extensively in my kitchen. Best known for its perfect marriage with tomatoes, basil is also scrumptious tossed with steamed summer vegetables. The more robust Thai and cinnamon basils are perfect paired up with chilli and garlic.

Basil is best eaten as soon after picking as possible. For the most intense flavour, add basil just before the end of the cooking process. When exposed to heat for too long, its oils dissipate. For salads, I find the basil flavour is maximised if I mush it into the dressing and let it steep for a while, rather than just tossing the whole leaves straight onto the salad.

Purists insist that basil should never be cut with a knife and should only be torn by hand. I disagree. Although I do often tear leaves, I also love using delicate ribbons of finely sliced basil – and it tastes just as good as 'torn' basil. Have a look at page 237 to see how to slice a basil *chiffonade*.

Harvesting, buying and storing basil

Wait until the basil plant is a decent size before harvesting the leaves. Once it starts forming flowers, it will stop producing new leaves. It is the leaves you want so whenever you see a flower forming, pinch it off about four to six leaf nodes down from the flower. This will encourage a bushier plant.

Buy basil that is bright green – avoid any with black edges or leaves. Basil does not dry well and loses its flavour quickly. (The exception to this is perennial basil, which does dry better than other varieties.) For long-term storage of basil, tear up the leaves, layer them in a sterilised bottle (see page 239) and cover with olive oil. I use the resulting basil-flavoured oil for salad dressing. As long as the leaves remain covered with oil, they will last for months. Another option is to blend basil with olive oil until it forms a thick paste. Freeze this in ice trays until solid, then transfer to zip lock bags. Add whole cubes to soups or defrost to use in salad dressings.

- 2 tablespoons grated palm sugar
- 2 tablespoons light soy sauce
- 2 tablespoons sesame oil
- juice of ¼ lime
- 2 tablespoons rice vinegar
- 1 teaspoon Japanese chilli (see page 250)

COLESLAW

- 3 cups finely sliced red and green cabbage
- 5 spring onions, sliced
- 2 carrots, julienned
- 10 baby corn, sliced
- 30 snow peas, stringed and cut in half crossways
- ½ cup basil, roughly shredded
- ¼ cup coriander, roughly shredded
- 1 cup roasted cashew nuts
- oil for deep-frying
- rice vermicelli noodles

SERVES 4

Asian crunchy coleslaw

Once you have tasted this salad with its fresh, herby flavour, you will find it difficult to go back to coleslaw made with mayonnaise. This coleslaw is all about texture and taste. The crunchiness of the fresh vegetables is complemented by the crisp noodles. And the dressing is sublime. Mix it with the noodles and vegetables just before serving as the vermicelli will absorb the dressing and if you leave it for any length of time, it will go soggy.

To make the dressing, mix all the ingredients together, whisking until the sugar has dissolved. Set aside.

To make the coleslaw, mix the vegetables, herbs and cashew nuts together in a bowl. Heat the oil in a medium-sized pot. Cut the noodles into roughly 10 cm lengths, holding them over a bowl so they don't scatter. Test to see if the oil is hot enough by adding small pieces of noodle. When the noodle immediately puffs up and rises to the surface, the oil is ready. Add the noodles in small bunches (they triple in size as they fry). As they puff and rise to the surface, scoop them out with a slotted spoon and drain on paper towels.

Mix the vegetables and the fried noodles together, crushing the noodles lightly so they are well mixed with the vegetables. Add the dressing just before serving, tossing until thoroughly mixed.

- **2 cups packed fresh basil**
- **⅓ cup pine nuts or walnuts**
- **3 medium-sized garlic cloves, minced**
- **½ cup extra virgin olive oil**
- **½ cup Parmesan cheese**
- **salt and black pepper**

Basil pesto

Making pesto is a good way to extend basil's life. It can also be frozen, but skip the cheese. When you want to use it, defrost and only then mix in the grated cheese. You can also replace the pine nuts with walnuts.

Combine the basil leaves with the pine nuts in a food processor. Pulse a few times. (If you are using whole walnuts instead of pine nuts, pulse them a few times first, before adding the basil.) Add the garlic, pulse a few times more.

With the food processor running, add the olive oil in a slow stream. Scrape the sides down and pulse a few more times. Add the cheese (freshly grated Parmesan or Pecorino) and pulse again until well blended. Season to taste. Scoop into sterilised bottles (see page 239) and cover the surface with olive oil. Store in the fridge.

Bangkok chicken and chilli with Thai basil

Bread and cereal are not part of Asian cuisine. We were based in Bangkok for a while and would often eat this dish for breakfast. It is so simple and easy to make yet it tastes complex and layered. Whenever I cook rice for an evening dish, I make more than I need so that I can quickly whip up stir-fried rice the next day – delicious for breakfast.

Heat the oil in a wok until it shimmers. Add the garlic and stir-fry briefly. Add the hot chilli, stir-frying for about 15 seconds, then add the chicken. Stir-fry until it has changed colour, about 1 to 2 minutes. Add the fish sauce, water and soy sauce, and stir until well combined. Add the sugar and let the mixture bubble for about a minute. Add the basil leaves and mild chillies, and stir briskly for about 15 seconds, until the basil begins to wilt. Serve over jasmine rice.

V Vegetarian option: replace the chicken with baby eggplant, sliced in half lengthways, and replace the fish sauce with salt to taste.

BANGKOK CHICKEN AND CHILLI WITH THAI BASIL

- 1 tablespoon peanut oil
- 1 tablespoon chopped garlic
- 1 tablespoon finely diced fresh hot red chilli
- 2 chicken breasts, cut into bite-sized pieces
- 2 tablespoons fish sauce
- 1 tablespoon water
- 1 teaspoon dark soy sauce
- 1 tablespoon brown sugar
- ½ cup Thai basil leaves (if unavailable, use normal basil leaves)
- 2 mild red chillies, sliced into long thin strips

SERVES 2

Green Goddess salmon, mango and avocado pear salad

In 1994, in San Francisco, three momentous events happened in my life: I gave up smoking, Keith and I tied the knot and I ate at Alice Waters' legendary Chez Panisse restaurant. It was a sublime birthday present meal. Alice Waters was way ahead of her time with her fresh, seasonal approach to cooking. Her Green Goddess dressing is a perfect example. This seasonal salad, lush with basil and other fresh summer herbs, is inspired by my meal at Chez Panisse.

GREEN GODDESS DRESSING

- ½ ripe avocado pear
- 3 tablespoons rice vinegar
- 1 small garlic clove, finely diced
- 1 oil-packed anchovy, finely chopped
- 1 teaspoon lemon juice
- ½ teaspoon lime juice
- ¼ teaspoon sugar
- ¾ cup olive oil
- ¼ cup cream
- 3 tablespoons flat leaf parsley, chopped
- 2 tablespoons dill, chopped
- 2 tablespoons coriander, chopped
- 1 tablespoon basil, chopped
- 3 spring onions, finely chopped
- salt and pepper

To make the dressing, blend the first 7 ingredients in a food processor until coarsely puréed. With the processor running, add the oil slowly through the top. Transfer the mixture to a bowl and whisk in the cream. Add all the herbs and the spring onion and whisk to combine. Season with salt and pepper to taste. Cover and refrigerate for 3 hours. Before serving, let the dressing stand at room temperature for a short while and give it a quick final whisk.

To make the salad, roast the pine nuts and cumin seeds in a cast iron frying pan over high heat, stirring often until the pine nuts are evenly browned. Add the chilli, stir through and tip the mixture into a small bowl.

Tear the lettuce leaves and spread onto a large serving platter. Peel the avocado and mango, cut into small chunks and toss over the lettuce. Scatter the rest of the ingredients evenly over the salad and sprinkle the pine nut mixture on top. Serve with Green Goddess dressing.

(This recipe is adapted from *Chez Panisse Vegetables*, William Morrow Cookbooks.)

V Vegetarian option: using 4 eggs make 2 thin omelettes. Roll these up, slice them into strips and substitute for the smoked salmon. When making the dressing, leave out the anchovy.

SALAD

- ¼ cup pine nuts
- 1 tablespoon cumin seeds
- 1 teaspoon Japanese chilli (see page 250)
- 1 large colander cos lettuce
- 1 avocado pear
- 1 small mango (or half a large one)
- 1 wheel of feta cheese, crumbled
- 15 cherry tomatoes
- ½ cup basil leaves, roughly torn
- 100 g smoked salmon, shredded

SERVES 4 AS A STARTER OR
SIDE DISH

BEANS

While beans might be quite boring on the supermarket shelf, home-grown beans are another story. For starters there are so many colours to choose from: purple, white, red, yellow and green. Then there's the choice of sizes: from slender French filet beans to fat runner beans with their neon pink seeds. And last of all, after enjoying the freshness of beans throughout summer, there is the quiet satisfaction of growing and harvesting beans to dry for winter stews.

Young French beans can be steamed, stir-fried, microwaved or eaten raw. Young runner beans can be eaten pod and all, but must be cooked first. Older ones need to be shelled, as the pods become tough and fibrous. Freshly shelled runner beans can be cooked and eaten whole, or puréed to make a dip.

Harvesting, buying and storing beans

The more beans you pick, the more they will produce. Rather use scissors to snip the beans off the stalk – if you pull them you risk damaging the plant. French beans produce for a shorter period of time than runner beans. French beans are best picked young, before the bean starts forming in the pod.

To harvest dried beans for winter use, leave them on the plant until fully mature. When the pods are dry and the beans rattle inside, they are ready to be shelled. The quickest way to shell large quantities of beans is to place them on a sack and beat them with a stick until the pods are broken up. Dried beans should be stored in an airtight container, with a few bay leaves added to the bottle to prevent any insects from eating them.

When shopping, look for beans that are crisp, green and whole. Avoid ones with big bumps as this indicates that they are overripe and past their best. Fresh green beans freeze very well. Blanch them before freezing (see page 236).

Thai red curry with pork and vegetables

I love the Thai style of eating a curry, where the dish is served in two separate bowls: one for curry and the other for rice. It is eaten by scooping up a spoonful of rice, which is then dipped into the creamy curry. Most Thai curries are quite liquid and by serving them this way, the rice doesn't become waterlogged by the curry sauce.

Made with loads of red chillies, Thai red curry paste is one of the hottest. Try making your own paste (the recipe is on page 227) rather than using a store-bought one, as the flavours are far fresher, punchier and more complex. Crunchy, fresh green beans complement this feisty curry perfectly.

- 2 tablespoons peanut oil
- 2 tablespoons red curry paste
- 2 cm fresh ginger, peeled and finely chopped
- 3 garlic cloves, diced
- 2 x 400 ml can coconut cream
- 30 green beans
- 500 g pork fillet, cut into thin strips
- 10 baby corn, cut in half
- 2 tablespoons Thai fish sauce
- 2 teaspoons grated palm sugar
- juice of ½ lime
- 1 long red chilli

SERVES 4

Heat the peanut oil in a wok over high heat until shimmering. Add the curry paste and cook for a couple of minutes, mashing it into the oil. Add the ginger and garlic and cook for further 30 seconds. Add the coconut cream and bring to the boil. Cook for 2 to 3 minutes until it thickens slightly, stirring until it is well mixed.

Top and tail the beans, and cut into 3 cm long pieces. Add the beans, pork strips, baby corn, fish sauce and sugar to the wok. Simmer for 5 to 6 minutes. Add the lime juice and taste. Adjust the seasoning by adding more sugar, lime juice or fish sauce if necessary.

Deseed the chilli, cut into thin strips and scatter over the curry. Serve with jasmine rice.

V Vegetarian option: replace the pork with 800 g full-bodied mushrooms, such as porcini or shiitake, thickly sliced. Replace the fish sauce with salt to taste.

Kalanga nut baked fish with almond and bean salad

FISH

- bunch fresh parsley
- 3 cloves garlic, diced
- salt to taste
- 1 tablespoon lemon juice
- 4 deboned trout
- 1 cup flour
- 2 teaspoons salt
- 2 teaspoons chilli powder
- 1 cup pure peanut butter (no salt or sugar added)
- 1 lemon cut into quarters

SALAD

- 1 cup beans
- 20 yellow and red cherry tomatoes
- ½ cup slivered almonds
- 3 tablespoons olive oil
- 1 tablespoon balsamic vinegar reduction (such as Black Gold)
- 2 tablespoons dukkah (see page 230)
- 1 wheel crumbled feta cheese

SERVES 4

The first time I left South Africa as an adult, I travelled to what was then Zaire. A friend and I spent several months exploring the craters of live volcanoes, coming eyeball to eyeball with gorillas and climbing the Mountains of the Moon.

The food was equally adventurous. One memorable meal was eaten while sitting on the banks of Lake Albert, on the border of Uganda. Whole *capitaine* fish was smothered in a paste made from kalanga nuts, a groundnut similar to peanuts, and baked over a fire. The oil cooked off, leaving a crunchy nutty crust with moist, delicious fish inside. Here is my version.

FISH

Preheat the oven to 240°C. Chop 4 tablespoons of parsley and mix it with the garlic, salt and lemon juice. Wash the fish and pat dry. Divide the parsley mixture evenly amongst the fish, placing it in the belly cavity.

Mix the flour, salt and chilli powder together on a plate. Pat the fish dry and, using your hands, rub a thin layer of peanut butter over each one, completely covering it. Dip the fish into the seasoned flour, covering the peanut butter evenly. Place the fish on a rack set over a baking tray and bake for 20 to 30 minutes, until the peanut butter crust is browned and crisp. Serve topped with parsley and a lemon quarter.

SALAD

Steam the beans until just cooked and place in ice water until cool. Drain them, dry well and scatter in a serving bowl with the tomatoes. Roast the almonds in a cast iron pan until browned then add to the salad bowl.

Whisk the olive oil and balsamic vinegar reduction together. Add the dukkah and mix well. Toss the salad with the dressing and sprinkle the feta cheese on top.

V Vegetarian option: mix together the garlic, chopped parsley, lemon juice, chilli powder and peanut butter. Add salt to taste. Spread this mixture evenly over the surface of 4 large portobello mushrooms, filling the cavity. Place stuffing side up on a baking tray and sprinkle with bread crumbs. Bake at 230°C until the mushrooms are cooked and the topping crispy.

Salted beans

Salt was once such a precious commodity that wars were fought over its production and possession. For centuries it has been used as a preservative – the micro organisms that attack our food cannot survive in a salty environment. This old-fashioned French recipe is a useful one as you can continually add harvested beans to the pot. It is best to use fresh young beans.

- non-iodised salt
- fresh beans

Put a layer of salt (use kosher or non-iodised salt) at the bottom of a sterilised earthenware crock or glass jar (see page 239). Wash and dry the beans. Remove the stems and strings and slice them in half lengthways. Place them in a layer on top of the salt. Use a wooden spoon to push them down firmly. Add another layer of salt on top. As a rough measure you should add 100 grams of salt for every 300 grams of beans.

In a couple of days, when you have harvested more beans, repeat this process. Continue layering salt and beans, finishing with a layer of salt. Cover and place in a cool spot. In time, brine will form, which keeps the beans in a salty environment. Once a month or so, check the surface and scoop off any film that appears. In winter, when green beans are long gone from the garden, scoop out enough beans for a meal and rinse them well. Soak them for 2 hours before cooking.

Beetroot

Beetroot is a fantastic vegetable to grow in a small garden. It is fast-growing and while the root is developing, the leaves can be eaten in salads and stir-fries. Although most recipes call for beetroot to be peeled, I often don't peel my small home-grown ones, as they are so tender. Beetroot can handle all stages of cooking – from raw and crunchy, to being roasted until its flavours caramelise into something completely different.

Harvesting, buying and storing beetroot

Beetroots can be harvested once they reach about 5 cm in diameter. If you leave them in the ground too long, they become woody and fibrous. Cut the leafy tops off immediately after harvesting otherwise they will continue to pull nutrients out of the root. But leave a few centimetres of stem to prevent the colour from bleeding.

Try to buy beetroots that have already had their leaves removed. Beetroots keep well on a vegetable rack for a couple of weeks and will keep even longer if left unwashed.

- 3 large beetroots
- 1 large grapefruit
- ¼ cup mint leaves
- ¼ cup orange juice
- 1 teaspoon white balsamic vinegar
- salt and pepper, to taste
- 2 tablespoons olive oil
- 2 spring onions, sliced
- rose petals for garnishing

SERVES 4

Roast beetroot with mint, grapefruit and rose petals

Roasting beetroot brings out its sweet earthiness — you can almost taste the goodness of the soil in which it grew. This seductive salad is a visual delight with the crimson beetroot contrasted by bright green mint and zesty grapefruit, topped with sultry rose petals.

Preheat the oven to 200°C. Cut the stems off the beetroot, leaving 2 cm at the top of each. Wrap them individually in foil, leaving the stems sticking out. Place on a baking tray and bake in the oven for 1½ to 2 hours. Stick a knife into them to see if they are tender. When cool, rub the skins off and cut into chunks.

Peel the grapefruit, remove the white pith and break into segments. Toss in a bowl with finely chopped mint and the beetroot chunks.

Whisk freshly squeezed orange juice, white balsamic vinegar, salt, pepper and olive oil together until blended. Add the spring onions and mix through. Pour this over the beetroot salad and mix well. Transfer to a pretty serving platter and decorate with rose petals.

- 6 medium beetroots
- 200 ml brown vinegar
- 200 ml red wine
- 1 teaspoon salt
- 1 tablespoon peppercorns (optional)

Bottled beetroot

With its ruby red pickling liquid, this has to be one of the most beautiful of all bottled vegetables on a pantry shelf. For flavour variations, add some herbs and spices, such as fresh mint and cumin seeds, to the vinegar before bringing to the boil.

Place the beetroots in a pot and just cover with water. Boil for about 25 minutes until softened. Remove the beetroots and reserve the water. Peel them if they have thick skins. Cut the beetroots into pieces that will fit into your bottles.

Measure 400 ml of the beetroot water and add it to a pot with the vinegar, wine, salt and peppercorns. Boil for 5 minutes. Add the beetroot pieces and bring back to the boil. Turn off the heat and ladle the beetroot into sterilised bottles (see page 239) making sure they are covered with liquid. Seal and store in your pantry.

CHILLIES

Chillies are one of the easiest vegetables to grow. They also add bright splashes of colour to the vegetable garden from mid-summer onwards. There is such a variety of chillies to choose from, with flavours ranging from sweet and piquant to mouth-blistering. I once grew a chilli called Scotch Bonnet. It was so hot that all it needed to set your mouth alight was a mere touch to the tip of the tongue with a toothpick that had been stuck inside one of the chillies. The resulting mouthful of fire brought tears to the eyes of even the most hardened of chilli-heads.

Chillies can be cooked in a variety of ways: slow roasted to bring out sweet depths of flavour; flame-grilled to add smoky depth to a dish; or diced and stir-fried for a sizzling zing. Just remember — it is the white membrane around the seeds that makes a chilli hot, so when you de-seed it you need to get rid of this too. If you do eat a chilli that is too hot, quickly eat a teaspoon of sugar. The taste receptors for chilli and sugar are in the same place and the sweetness cancels out the fire. This is much more effective than milk or anything else I have tried. It is probably the reason why I love eating chocolate after a fiery dish.

Harvesting and storing chillies

Chillies should be harvested regularly to encourage further fruiting. Cut the fruit off rather than pulling it. If you leave some on the bush, they will ripen, changing colour and intensifying in heat and flavour as time goes by. Handle hot chillies with care and, if you are processing in bulk, use a mask and gloves. I've had chilli burn on my hands for days after forgetting to use gloves.

Chillies dry easily and a decorative and practical way of storing them is to string them together using a needle and thread. Thread fresh chillies by their stems and gather them into what the Mexicans call a *ristra*. Whenever you need one, pick it off the string. Once you have dried your chillies, try crushing them and combining different varieties with other spices for interesting mixes and rubs.

- 2 tablespoons peanut oil
- 4 large dried hot red chillies, cut into thick strips
- 1 cup unsalted cashew nuts
- 3 large cloves garlic, diced into small cubes
- 1 cm fresh ginger, finely chopped
- 2 stalks lemon grass, finely chopped
- 4 filleted, skinless chicken breasts, cut into small strips
- 3 carrots, julienned
- 20 snow or sugar snap peas, strings removed
- 1 tablespoon mirin
- 2 tablespoons teriyaki sauce
- 2 teaspoons dark soy sauce
- 2 tablespoons sweet chilli sauce
- 2 teaspoons sesame oil

SERVES 4

Chengdu chicken and cashew nut stir-fry

I only started enjoying hot food after I first travelled in Southeast Asia. It crept up on me and before I knew it I went from not being able to tolerate even a mild curry to being a chilli-head.

I was lucky I visited Chengdu after becoming smitten with chilli. Sichuan is China's spiciest province and Chengdu, its capital, is the Kingdom of Chilli. There is no mild choice here; dishes are either hot or flaming. Chillies — fresh, fried, dried, powdered, stewed and pickled — are part of every dish. Even at Kentucky Fried Chicken you'll find some chilli under the Colonel's secret sauce. Many hot dishes also feature Sichuan pepper, a tiny fruit not related to pepper at all, which leaves your tongue and lips disconcertingly numb. This hot dish is a tribute to Chengdu.

Heat the peanut oil in a wok until very hot. Add the chillies and cashew nuts and stir-fry quickly for 1 to 2 minutes. Add the garlic, ginger and lemon grass, and stir-fry for 30 to 40 seconds.

Add the chicken and stir-fry until it changes colour. Add the carrots and snow peas, stir-frying for another 1 to 2 minutes. Add the remaining ingredients and cook until the sauce has thickened slightly.

Serve with jasmine rice or noodles.

V Vegetarian option: replace the chicken with diced tofu.

Shiitake noodles

Shiitake mushrooms originate from China, although they are commonly known by their Japanese name. They are meatier and richer tasting than many other mushrooms and are the perfect foil for the zing of fresh red chilli.

Fresh ones are available but dried ones are just as tasty – and are half the price. Dried shiitake need to be soaked in boiling water until soft before you use them. The tasty soaking water can be added to this dish instead of plain water. Strain it first as it might be gritty.

One other thing to know about shiitake: their stems are tougher and take longer to cook than the rest of the mushroom. When preparing them, remove the stems and use them in another dish requiring a longer cooking time.

- 3 tablespoons butter
- 2 tablespoons olive oil
- 3 garlic cloves, diced
- I fresh red chilli, sliced
- about 15 shiitake mushroom caps, thickly sliced
- 180 g slender green beans
- 2 tablespoons flour
- 1½ cups water (or mushroom-soaking water)
- 3 tablespoons teriyaki sauce
- I teaspoon sesame oil
- pinch sugar
- ¼ cup chopped fresh parsley
- squeeze of lime juice

SERVES 4

Melt the butter and oil in a frying pan. Add the garlic and chilli and cook for 2 minutes. Add the mushrooms, stirring quickly to make sure that they are evenly coated with the butter and oil, and cook for 2 minutes. Cut the beans into short lengths, add and cook for 1 minute more.

Using a flour shaker, sprinkle the flour into the pan and stir to combine it with the butter and oil – if need be, add a little more butter – and cook for a minute. Remove from heat and slowly add the water, stirring all the time to prevent lumps from forming. Mix until smooth.

Return to heat and add the teriyaki sauce, sesame oil and sugar. Bring to the boil, stirring occasionally, until the sauce thickens slightly.

Remove from heat and add the parsley and lime juice. Serve over noodles.

- 2 red bell peppers
- 10 red jalapeno chillies
- 1½ cups white vinegar
- 1 tablespoon lemon pips
- 6 cups sugar
- ⅓ cup lemon juice

Jane's hot diggedy chilli jelly

When I first started my vegetable garden, I grew over 20 varieties of chillies. Faced with this abundance, I began experimenting with chilli recipes. My hot diggedy chilli jelly soon became a favourite amongst friends. So much so that after I had been away for nine months, a friend greeted me with, 'Oh, good you're back – when are you going to make some chilli jelly?' Here's the recipe, so my friends can make it themselves now!

Cut the peppers into quarters and remove the white inner ribs. Purée the chillies and peppers in a food processor. Combine the purée and vinegar in a large pot and bring to the boil. Boil rapidly for 10 minutes, stirring occasionally. (Be warned: the steam is pungent and it will make your eyes sting and the whole house pong of vinegar and chillies.)

Tie the lemon pips in a muslin bag, or put them inside a tea strainer that closes, and add them to the pot. (The lemon pips contain plenty of pectin – the stuff that makes jelly gel.) Now add the sugar and lemon juice, stirring well until the sugar has completely dissolved. Bring back to the boil and cook until it wrinkles when tested (see page 240). Remove the lemon pips and pour the jelly into sterilised bottles (see page 239) and seal.

My favourite way of eating chilli jelly is with Philadelphia cream cheese spread onto hot croissants. Try it!

SALAD

- mixed salad greens
- 2 slices watermelon
- 2 wheels creamy feta, diced
- ¼ cup peppadew, finely sliced
- ¼ cup pine nuts
- I teaspoon Japanese chilli (see page 250)

DRESSING

- 3 tablespoons extra virgin olive oil
- I tablespoon Cape gooseberry balsamic vinegar

SERVES 4 AS A STARTER OR SIDE DISH

- ½ cup rice vinegar
- I cup sugar
- ½ cup water
- I teaspoon salt
- 3 tablespoons garlic, finely diced
- 2 tablespoons hot red chillies, finely chopped
- I tablespoon fish sauce
- I tablespoon lime juice

Turkish watermelon and feta salad

When Keith was young he lived in Turkey for a number of years. He introduced me to his favourite Turkish summer snack: a chunk of fresh red watermelon popped into the mouth followed by a cube of salty, creamy feta cheese. If you haven't discovered this combination yet, you are in for a taste sensation that shouts 'summer!'

The following recipe has evolved from that simple snack, with the peppadew and chilli adding a welcome bite. But if you don't feel like making the salad, simply chop up cubes of watermelon and feta, arm your guests with mini forks and get out of the way.

To make the salad, place a colander of lettuce, watercress and rocket onto a serving platter. Skin the watermelon, remove the pips and dice into bite-sized pieces. Scatter the watermelon, feta and peppadew evenly over the top of the leaves.

Dry-fry the pine nuts in a cast iron pan until they just turn brown. Add the Japanese chilli and stir through. Sprinkle over the top of the salad.

To make the dressing, whisk the oil and balsamic vinegar together until well blended. (I love the Cape gooseberry variety, but you can use any other light berry balsamic reduction.) Drizzle over the salad just before serving.

Thai sweet chilli sauce

I use this sauce extensively in my kitchen. It is one of those magic ingredients that you can always rely on when you are looking to add 'something' to a dish but you are not quite sure what.

Combine the first 6 ingredients in a medium saucepan. Bring to the boil, stirring to dissolve the sugar. Reduce heat and simmer for about 20 minutes, until it thickens to a syrup. Add the fish sauce and lime juice and simmer for a couple of minutes more. Pour into a sterilised bottle (see page 239) and seal. This will keep for up to 6 months in your pantry – if it lasts that long!

EDIBLE FLOWERS

Flowers can make a dish sing. And there are plenty of flowers in your garden, other than the well-known nasturtium, that can be popped onto a plate. Calendula, California poppy, carnation, cornflower, daylily (*Hemerocallis* species), fuchsia, herb flowers, hibiscus, lavender, pansy, pelargonium and rose are all easy to grow and safe to eat.

Harvesting, storing and using edible flowers

Before eating flowers, make sure you have identified them correctly – there are some poisonous ones out there. It is best to eat just the petals of edible flowers, rather than the whole flower as the pollen of some blooms can cause hay fever and allergies. If you tend to suffer from allergies, start by eating just one or two flowers to make sure you don't have a reaction.

It is preferable to eat flowers that you have grown yourself, as you know they are free of pesticides. Harvest them early in the morning, before the heat of the sun wilts them. Place whole flowers in a bowl of water in the fridge until you are ready to use them. This will keep them fresh for a day or two.

There are many ways to use edible flowers: toss them on top of salads; freeze them in individual ice cubes and add to drinks; stuff larger ones with cream cheese and chives; add them to jellies; mix them into icing sugar when baking; and make flowered butter with a variety of herb flowers. One of my favourite ways of using flowers in the kitchen is to make herbal flower sugar (see page 101).

- 1 large colander strongly scented flowers and leaves
- 2 cinnamon sticks
- 1 vanilla pod
- 1 lump frankincense

Delicious garden incense

Walking in my garden early one summer morning, with the fragrance of rose pelargonium, lavender and mint around me, I wondered how I could bottle that scent. So I started experimenting with making incense. After drying the leaves I blended them with some spices and frankincense. I placed a large pinch of the incense on an oil burner above a candle and waited to see if I would smell anything. The result was a combination of sacred scent and grandma's cooking.

When blending the Delicious garden incense, I choose from what is in season and this includes roses, lavender, rosemary, various types of pelargonium, mint, lemon verbena and lemon grass. Frankincense is readily available at Indian spice shops.

This is not an overpowering, cloying incense. It is quiet and subtle, yet it creeps around corners and fills the room with its delicate presence.

Heat the oven to 100°C. Strip the leaves off their stems (see preparing herbs on page 237). Chop the leaves and flowers in batches in a food processor until fine. Spread them onto a flat baking tray and bake for 3 to 4 hours, turning and fluffing occasionally to ensure that they dry evenly. Turn the heat off and leave in the oven overnight. Tip into a large bowl when you are ready to mix the incense.

In a blender, chop the cinnamon sticks and vanilla pod finely and add to the dried leaves. Using a pestle and mortar, crush the frankincense to a powder. Add to the leaves and mix well. Store in the freezer in zip lock bags with all the air removed (see page 238).

To use, fill the bowl of an oil burner with the incense and light the candle. Revel in the heady fragrance. (There is no need to add any oil to the incense – the natural oils in the spices and herbs will be released when heated.)

- 4 ripe yellow cling peaches, cut in slices with the pip removed
- lemon verbena sugar (see page 101)
- 500 ml cream

SERVES 4

Seared peaches with lemon verbena sugar and cream

The seared, caramelised bits of fresh sweet peaches, take this from being a plain fruit dessert to something more special. Mangoes make a yummy alternative. Fruit can also be seared over a fire – just make sure the grid is well oiled.

This dish can easily be turned into a main course. Mix fish with fruit on skewers and pop on a braai. Or for a salad, chop the seared peaches and mix with shredded smoked chicken. Serve on a bed of rocket and mixed greens.

Heat a ridged cast iron grill pan over high heat. Sprinkle the peaches with the lemon verbena sugar. When it is hot, brush the grill pan with oil and place the peaches, flat side down, in the pan. Cook for 2 to 3 minutes until brown grill lines are seared across the fruit and they have softened slightly. Using tongs, remove them from the pan and place on a platter. Serve with whipped cream mixed with lemon verbena sugar.

Herbal flower sugars

I use these delicately flavoured sugars in herbal teas, sprinkled on fruit, whipped up with cream and to flavour icing. Experiment with different combinations or use only one herb, such as lemon verbena, for specific flavour.

Gather a large colander of fragrant herbs, such as lemon verbena, rose geranium, mint and lavender. To add flashes of colour to the sugar, pick a small bowl of cornflowers, deep red roses and pansies.

Wash and dry the herbs and flowers well, using a salad spinner and then dishcloths. Remove the central part of the flowers, keeping just the petals. Chop the petals into small pieces and set aside. Strip off the herbs' leaves, discarding any woody stems. Using a food processor, chop the herbs in stages until fine.

Measure the herbs and for every cup of chopped herbs, add two cups of sugar. You can use brown or white sugar for different tastes and textures. Add some vanilla or cinnamon for a little extra interest. Mix together well. Using a blender, blend one cup of the mixture at a time until the sugar is fine and smooth. Mix the petals through with a spoon and store the sugar in airtight bottles.

As an alternative, use whole herb leaves, such as lemon verbena. Layer the leaves with the sugar in a bottle. This preserves the leaves, which can then be used whole at a later stage, and flavours the sugar at the same time.

Note: you don't have to dry the herbs or flowers beforehand. Using fresh ones makes the sugar quite moist but far more flavourful and as sugar is a natural preservative, it will keep for months.

- large colander herbs
- small bowl edible flower petals
- sugar

SUMMER SQUASH

The first zucchini and patty pans of the season are so exciting. But by
the middle of squash season I am giving away basketfuls and by the end I
don't want to see another squash for quite a while. Zucchini, patty pans,
gem squash and the rest of this mid-summer family are prolific bearers
and you really need only one or two bushes for a small family. However, I
like variety so I always land up with far more than just two bushes and far
more squash than we can possibly eat. Luckily these vegetables are very
versatile in the kitchen. From simple steaming to being stuffed and baked,
summer squash can be used in an endless variety of dishes.

Harvesting, buying and storing summer squash

Most summer squash are tastiest when picked quite small. Rather use a pair of
scissors to cut them off the bush to avoid damaging the plant. Frequent picking
encourages more to grow. When buying squash, look for small firm ones with a
vivid colour. If the skin looks dull or if they are soft and limp, avoid them.

One of the best ways to extend their shelf life is to wipe unwashed squash
with olive oil. Store them on a shelf in the pantry or a similar cool dark spot,
making sure they are not touching one another. The film of oil prevents air from
reaching the skin and stops any moulds or fungi from growing. Reapply the
oil about once a week and check regularly for any soft ones, which should be
discarded. Softer-skinned squash, such as patty pans, will keep for about 6 weeks
and harder-skinned varieties, like gem squash, will keep for up to 3 months.

- 500 g cake flour
- 1 tablespoon baking powder
- ½ teaspoon salt
- 60 g chilled butter
- 4 cups grated squash (deseeded if necessary)
- 125 g grated cheddar cheese
- 2 eggs, beaten
- toasted sunflower seeds for sprinkling

Quick bread with summer squash

One late summer we stayed with our friends David and Gill in southern England. We went for long walks in forests, picked wild brambleberries and ate plenty of pub lunches. David loved making bread and every morning we would wake up to the smell of a freshly baked loaf. This bread is adapted from one of his recipes for an apple and cheese loaf. I tried it one year when the summer squash harvest grew completely out of hand. The squash makes the bread moist and flavourful and the cheese adds a scrumptious crunchy crust. This bread is not only delicious but is also very quick to make.

Preheat the oven to 180°C. Grease 2 medium loaf tins with oil. Sift the flour, baking powder and salt together into a large bowl. Quickly rub the butter into the flour with your fingers until well mixed – it should resemble breadcrumbs. Stir the grated squash and cheese into the flour. Add the beaten eggs and mix well.

   Spoon the batter into the loaf tins, pushing it into the corners and smoothing the top. Sprinkle with sunflower seeds and bake for 1½ to 2 hours until it is golden brown. It is ready when a skewer stuck into the middle comes out clean. Turn onto a wire rack to cool.

DRESSING

- ¼ cup pomegranate concentrate
- ¼ cup mango juice
- 2 tablespoons olive oil
- 1 tablespoon whole-grain mustard
- salt and pepper to taste
- 1 red onion, finely sliced

SALAD

- 5 courgettes and 5 patty pans, cut into bite-sized chunks
- 1 small cucumber, finely sliced
- ½ cup basil leaves, shredded
- 1 cup cherry tomatoes
- ½ mango, cubed
- 1 fresh red chilli, chopped

SERVES 4 AS A STARTER OR
SIDE DISH

Summer squash salad with basil and mango

I grew up with a mango tree in the garden. But they weren't the kind of fat, fibreless mangoes we can buy today. These were small with plenty of strings. The only way to eat them was to sit on the top step of the pool and get stuck in – then fall in the water afterwards to wash off the mango face.

Cold squash creates a delicious crunch in this colourful salad. Just make sure you don't overcook it – soggy cold squash doesn't work nearly as well! For a variation, slice the squash very finely, brush with olive oil and cook quickly in a ridged grill pan over a high heat. The seared lines add a caramelised flavour to the dish.

DRESSING

Whisk the first 5 ingredients together until smooth. Add the onion and leave to stand for an hour.

SALAD

Steam the squash until just cooked and still crunchy. Leave to cool for 10 minutes. Transfer to a serving bowl and mix with the cucumber, basil and cherry tomatoes.

Add the mango and chilli to the salad dressing and stir through until well mixed. Pour over the salad and toss everything together until well coated. Serve with fresh olive bread.

Chao Leh fish soup

- 4 cups chicken stock
  (see page 232)
- 6 slices galangal
  (see page 250)
- 1 whole stalk lemon
  grass, bruised
- 2 fresh or dried Asian
  lime leaves
- 400 ml can coconut milk
- 1 tablespoon grated
  palm sugar
- pinch salt
- 2 to 3 chillies cut into
  big slices
- 1 tablespoon fish sauce
- 400 g firm white fish fillets,
  cut into bite-sized pieces
- 6 button mushrooms, sliced
- 3 yellow patty pans, cut
  into chunks
- 2 teaspoons lime juice
- 2 tablespoons coriander

SERVES 4

We spent a few weeks on Koh Lipe, a small island on the edge of the Tarutao National Marine Park, in the Andaman Sea southwest of Thailand. Surrounded by seas speckled with hundreds of coral reefs and abundant sea life, Koh Lipe is the only inhabited island in the group of 51 protected islands.

It is also home to a community of Chao Leh, or Sea Gypsies. These masters of the ocean took us on day trips to the uninhabited islands, where we spent hours exploring above and below the water. Arriving back hungry and sunburnt, their wives plied me with aloe vera and coconut oil for my skin, and a feast for our hungry tummies. This citrusy, spicy, coconutty soup is inspired by the Chao Leh.

Bring the stock to a boil in a medium-sized pot. Add the galangal, lemon grass and lime leaves. Simmer for 8 minutes. Add the coconut milk, sugar, salt, chillies and fish sauce, and simmer for a further 5 minutes. Add the fish, mushrooms and patty pans, and simmer gently until the fish is just cooked. Turn off the heat and add the lime juice.

Taste to see that there is good balance between the salty, sour and sweet flavours. Top with the coriander leaves and serve.

V Vegetarian option: use vegetable stock and replace the fish sauce with salt to taste. Substitute chunks of tofu for the fish.

Grilled zucchini in olive oil

This is a quick and easy way to preserve bountiful squash. I find they taste better chilled, so pop them in the fridge before eating. These are delicious with mature cheddar cheese.

- 1 kg zucchini
- 2 red onions, thinly sliced
- 2 tablespoons olive oil
- 2½ to 3 cups white wine vinegar
- few sprigs fresh oregano
- about 2 cups olive oil

Slice the zucchini in half lengthwise. Toss the onion and zucchini with 2 tablespoons of olive oil and spread onto baking trays. Grill for 5 to 10 minutes until just starting to brown.

Bring the vinegar to the boil and as soon as it starts bubbling, add the zucchini and onion. Cover and bring back to the boil. Cook for a minute then strain through a sieve.

Pack the zucchini and onion into hot, sterilised bottles (see page 239), adding sprigs of oregano and covering with olive oil as you go. Seal and store in a cool dark spot for about 2 to 3 weeks before eating, allowing the flavours to mature.

TOMATOES

I still remember standing in my garden and for the first time eating a tomato that I had grown from seeds I had saved. It was sublime. Not only because I had grown it myself – it just tasted so good! I have popped many ripe tomatoes into my mouth since then, but that first one was particularly special. Tomatoes are not only really good for you, they are also extraordinarily versatile in the kitchen.

Harvesting, buying and storing tomatoes

The best way to kill the texture and flavour of a vine-ripened tomato is to put it in the fridge. The cold temperature breaks down the cell walls, turning a crisp tomato into a mushy, mealy one. Rather store tomatoes in a vegetable drawer in your kitchen – you will taste the difference. When buying tomatoes be aware of this and look for a seller who does not refrigerate tomatoes.

Two tasty ways of preserving that delicious summer tomato taste is to dry or to bottle them. See pages 225 to 226 for some recipes for bottled tomatoes. Sun-dried tomatoes are often quite expensive, but with a little effort you can make your own (see page 120).

- 250 g rump steak
- olive oil
- 5 tablespoons dukkah
  (see page 230)
- 30 cherry tomatoes, halved
- pepper and herbal salt
  (see page 53)
- 4 medium-sized summer
  squash (yellow patty pans,
  courgettes)
- 4 sticks of Danish-style feta
  cheese, cubed
- balsamic reduction
- basil *chiffonade*

SERVES 2

Dukkah steak salad with cherry tomatoes and summer squash

Dukkah originates from Egypt but is now used in many Middle Eastern dishes. It is an addictive combination of roasted nuts and spices, ground into a coarse powder. I first ate it with crusty Turkish bread, dipped in olive oil, then in the spice mixture. And I was hooked. I now add dukkah to a wide variety of dishes. If you want to make your own, try my recipe on page 230.

Roasting cherry tomatoes at a low heat is a sublime way of cooking them as it sweetens and deepens their flavour. This dish can be served warm or made ahead and served at room temperature.

Rub the steak on both sides with olive oil. Sprinkle 2 tablespoons of dukkah over, pressing it firmly into the surface of the steak. Set aside.

Heat the oven to 160°C. Toss the cherry tomatoes with some olive oil, and herbal salt and pepper to taste. Place them cut side down on baking paper on a baking tray. Pop them in the oven and cook for 20 to 30 minutes.

While the tomatoes are cooking, slice the summer squash thinly and toss with olive oil. Heat a ridged cast iron pan over high heat. Cook the squash in a single layer, turning once, until they are softened, with dark grill lines. Remove and place in a serving bowl.

Heat a cast iron pan until hot and add a splash of olive oil. Cook the steak for 2 to 3 minutes on either side. Remove the steak from the heat and leave to stand for 10 minutes before slicing thinly.

Add the steak strips, roasted tomatoes (along with any liquid on the baking sheet), feta and 3 tablespoons of dukkah to the squash in the serving bowl. Drizzle with balsamic reduction and toss gently. Top with the basil chiffonade.

V Vegetarian option: leave out the steak and increase the amount of squash.

- 250 g Gorgonzola or other blue cheese
- ¾ cup full cream milk
- 1½ teaspoons chilli jelly (see page 92)
- 15 cherry tomatoes
- ¼ cup toasted pine nuts
- pasta for four
- fresh basil for serving

SERVES 4 (PEOPLE – NOT CATS)

Gatto Gorgonzola and cherry tomato pasta

In the early nineties we spent a few months in Italy. I loved shopping at the open-air markets, with their daily fresh produce, and at the many 'Mom and Pop' delis. There were very few supermarket chains and almost everything we ate was locally made, in season and fresh.

In those months I learnt plenty about pasta. Even the cats in Rome eat pasta. There are colonies of feral cats at the countless archaeological ruins. Every day they are fed leftover pasta, most often by muttering, bent-over, cat-loving crones.

For this dish use the best-tasting Gorgonzola you can find. I use Cremalat's Gorgonzola – soft and creamy with a rich taste.

Cut the cheese into pieces and melt over a low heat in a heavy-bottomed pot. Add the milk and chilli jelly and stir until well mixed. Add the cherry tomatoes and heat until the sauce just starts bubbling. Remove from the heat, stir in the pine nuts and serve with pasta, topped with basil.

SALAD

- 1 kg fish fillets
- olive oil
- salt and pepper to taste
- 1 large colander mixed greens
- 1 large mango, diced
- 2 avocado pears, diced
- 5 spring onions, sliced
- 500 g cherry tomatoes, halved
- 2 tablespoons black sesame seeds

DRESSING

- 3 cloves roasted garlic (see page 227)
- 1 teaspoon grated ginger
- 1 teaspoon brown sugar
- 2 teaspoons rice vinegar
- ½ cup chopped fresh coriander leaves
- 1 small fresh red chilli
- 1 large tomato, peeled (see page 236)
- 1 teaspoon sesame oil
- 1½ teaspoons lime juice
- ¼ cup peanut oil
- salt and pepper to taste

SERVES 4 AS A STARTER OR
SIDE DISH

Fish, mango and tomato salad

The first time I visited Sydney was in 1991. The next time I was there was in 2000. The difference was remarkable. In the intervening ten years the food scene had gone from ordinary to astounding. I ate swordfish steak at a seafood restaurant and it was served with mangoes and a sublime sauce. Although I asked for the recipe, it wasn't forthcoming.

Back home I experimented and came up with my own version, which has now eclipsed the Sydney one from my taste buds' memory. The first time I made this, I served it with swordfish steaks but swordfish has been over fished and is on SASSI's orange list (see www.wwfsass.co.za) for more information). Since swordfish is off the menu, choose any firm fish such as yellowtail or Cape salmon. Prawns or calamari would also work well.

SALAD

Brush the fish fillets with the olive oil and season with salt and pepper to taste. Grill for a few minutes on each side, until cooked. Leave to cool and then cut the fillets into bite-sized pieces.

Spread the greens onto a large platter. (I like using rocket, watercress and baby lettuce leaves.) Scatter the mango, avocado pear, spring onions and tomatoes evenly over the greens. Add the fish fillets to the salad and drizzle with the dressing. Sprinkle the sesame seeds on top.

DRESSING

Squeeze the roasted garlic cloves out of their skins and place with all the other ingredients in a processor. Blitz until smooth.

V Vegetarian option: replace the fish fillets with baby potatoes.

Sun-dried tomatoes

Roma tomatoes are a good choice as they are fleshy without too many pips. But you can use any tomatoes – even cherry tomatoes – as long as you choose ones that are of a similar size so that they dry at the same rate.

Cut the tomatoes in half (or if using larger ones, in slices) and place them on racks set over baking trays to catch any drips. Cover them loosely with cheesecloth to protect from bugs and then place outside in the sun.

Depending on the temperature, it will take anything from a couple of days to a week for them to dry. If you want to speed up the process, place them on the dashboard or front seat of your car and park it in the sun. They will dry in about two days! They will shrink quite a bit as they dry and will be ready when they are as pliable as a raisin, without any stickiness or wateriness.

Pack them into a zip lock bag and remove as much air as possible (see page 238). It is best to store them in the freezer – if there is too much moisture left in the tomatoes, they can go mouldy if stored in the fridge.

AUTUMN

MARCH 22 – JUNE 21

Autumn is a second spring when every leaf is a flower.
Albert Camus

As the leaves begin to turn orange, yellow and red, the nights become chillier and the days shorter. Potato, Jerusalem artichoke and walnut harvests are transformed into feasts in front of the fire. Cats come to cuddle on our laps and it is time to think about slower vegetables and warmer dishes. In our edible gardens the summer rush of abundance tails off as the cooler vegetables bed down, ready for winter. The sun loses its bite and it is the perfect time to be busy in the garden.

IN SEASON IN AUTUMN

Asian greens	Herbs	Rocket
Beans	Horseradish	Spinach
Beetroot	Jerusalem artichoke	Sweet potatoes
Cabbage	Kale	Swiss chard
Chillies	Lettuce	Walnuts
Eggplant	Parsnips	
Ginger	Potatoes	

EGGPLANT

By planting successive crops, you will continue to harvest healthy eggplant well into May. Growing from seed gives you a wide choice; from the glossy purple almost black ones, to speckled mauve and creamy white ones.

Eggplant is incredibly versatile in the kitchen and is a great meat substitute for vegetarians. It can be stuffed, sliced or grated; baked, fried or grilled. Many recipes call for eggplants to be salted before cooking to draw out the bitterness and reduce the amount of oil they absorb while cooking. I find with freshly picked home-grown varieties there is no need to do this, as they aren't bitter. Instead of wasting time salting, waiting and washing them, I use a good-quality olive oil that tastes great when absorbed by the eggplant. Eggplants soak up flavours like a sponge and are best paired with robust partners such as rosemary, garlic, onions and chillies.

Harvesting, buying and storing eggplant

Eggplants should be picked and bought when they are firm and feel heavy. An overripe eggplant will look dull and feel soft. Regular picking will encourage further fruiting. Younger fruit have less chance of tasting bitter. Fruit should be cut off – not pulled, as this will damage the plant. Freshly harvested eggplants taste the best but if you have to store them, keep in the crisper drawer of the fridge for up to 3 days.

- 2 large eggplants
- olive oil
- ½ cup peppadews, sliced
- 2 tablespoons peppadew liquid
- ½ cup mint, sliced
- 1 wheel feta, crumbled

SERVES 4 AS A STARTER

Eggplant rolls with peppadew, feta and mint

This recipe was inspired by none other than the Kitchen Goddess herself, Nigella Lawson. In her version, she uses hot chillies and lemon juice. Instead of chillies I prefer the sweet and hot, uniquely South African peppadews. Replacing the lemon juice with the delicious peppadew pickling liquid adds a further dimension to this dish. The resulting colour and flavourful combination of sweet red peppadew, salty white feta and fresh green mint, rolled up in a mellow roasted eggplant wrap is simply irresistible. These are great 'make ahead' party snacks. Serve on top of a bed of rocket.

Heat the oven to 200°C. Cut the eggplant lengthways into thin slices. (If it is not a freshly picked eggplant, salt it first – see page 238.) Brush both sides with olive oil and place in a single layer on a baking tray (use 2 if necessary). Bake until soft, about 12 to 15 minutes, and remove from the oven, leaving them to cool.

While the eggplant is cooking, mix the peppadew, peppadew liquid and mint in a bowl. Add the crumbled feta and mix through. Once the eggplant has cooled, work with one slice at a time. Place a spoon of mixture at one end and roll it up, securing with a toothpick. Repeat until they are all filled.

Eggplant preserved in olive oil

In most Italian markets you will find somebody selling tempting thick slices of roast eggplant mixed with olive oil and herbs. For me they are the essence of Italy. This versatile recipe is a great way to use up excess eggplants. They can be tossed in a salad, added to an antipasto platter, blended to create a dip, or layered with cheese and tomato on top of crusty bread. An added bonus is the yummy flavoured oil.

- 2 large eggplants, sliced into rounds
- olive oil
- 3 cloves garlic, sliced
- 1 large mild chilli, sliced into strips
- 1 tablespoon fresh oregano
- salt and pepper to taste
- olive oil for bottling

If necessary, salt and rinse the eggplant (see page 238). Toss with a generous dollop of olive oil, garlic, chilli, fresh oregano, and salt and pepper to taste. Spread out in a single layer in a large roasting pan. Bake at 200°C for 20 minutes until soft. Place in layers in sterilised bottles (see page 239), covering with olive oil. Shake gently to remove any air bubbles. It will keep in the fridge for up to 6 months.

Roast eggplant, tomato and mozzarella with balsamic vinegar

Roasting eggplants brings out their wonderful sweetness. Here, they are perfectly complemented by melted mozzarella, tomato, balsamic vinegar and fresh herbs. By layering the slices, the flavours blend together.

Heat the oven to 200°C. If it is not a freshly picked eggplant, salt it first (see page 238). Toss the eggplant and tomatoes with a generous dollop of olive oil, herbal salt and pepper to taste. Place the eggplant slices in a single layer on a baking tray and roast for 15 minutes. Add the tomatoes and cook for a further 15 minutes. Remove and leave to cool for 10 minutes.

  Create stacks of alternating eggplant, mozzarella and tomato, starting with a slice of eggplant, to create six stacks containing two slices of each. Use a metal or bamboo skewer to pierce a hole down the centre of each stack. Push sprigs of rosemary into the holes and place the stacks in the oven and bake until the mozzarella has melted. To serve, whisk the balsamic vinegar with the basil oil and drizzle over the stacks. Sprinkle with basil *chiffonade*.

ROAST EGGPLANT, TOMATO AND MOZZARELLA

- 2 large eggplants, sliced into 12 rounds (or 6 baby eggplants sliced in half)
- 4 large tomatoes sliced horizontally in thirds
- olive oil
- herbal salt to taste (see page 53)
- black pepper
- 400 g mozzarella cheese, sliced into twelve rounds
- stalks of fresh rosemary
- 1 tablespoon balsamic vinegar
- 2 tablespoons basil oil (see page 67)
- basil *chiffonade* (see page 237)

SERVES 6 AS A SIDE DISH
OR STARTER

GINGER

The first time I saw ginger growing wild was in Zanzibar. It is a beautiful plant with long strap-like green leaves and a mass of delicious rhizomes underground. Growing nearby was turmeric, with similar leaves and the brightest orange roots imaginable. I was inspired to try growing both in my non-Zanzibar climate. The ginger worked, the turmeric didn't.

Ginger is an essential part of what I call the holy trinity of my cooking: chilli, garlic and ginger. Ginger, with its sweet heat and fresh bite, adds a zing to any dish. Ginger can be juiced, chopped, diced, finely grated and stir-fried, or thickly sliced and slow roasted. For easy peeling of ginger, see page 236.

Harvesting, buying and storing ginger

You can harvest side shoots of ginger throughout the growing season but the bulk of the harvest is done after the leaves have died down, about eight to ten months after planting. When buying ginger look for plump rhizomes with unwrinkled skin.

Store fresh unpeeled ginger in a zip lock bag in the fridge for up to two months. For longer-term storage, peel the ginger and pop it into jars. Fill the jars with vodka, seal and place them in the freezer. They will keep for months and results in delicious ginger-flavoured vodka. Ginger also dries well. Peel fresh ginger, cut it into small slices and place on a rack in the sun for a few days until dry. Store in a bottle with a spice-grinder top and grind it into a simmering dish whenever that sharp, gingery flavour is needed.

- 1 kg sirloin steak, cut into chunks
- 1 large onion, cut into chunks
- 3 cloves garlic, peeled
- ½ cup raw peanuts
- 4 small hot chillies, chopped
- 1 tablespoon fresh ginger, chopped
- 1 teaspoon salt
- ½ teaspoon freshly ground black pepper
- ¼ cup peanut oil
- 2 more onions, cut into small chunks
- 1 cup roasted peanuts
- 1 cup flour

SERVES 4

Agadez grilled brochettes

I have never been to Timbuktu. But I have been to Agadez, which is not far away. Situated in the depths of the Sahara desert, it has been part of the camel caravan route for centuries.

We were there to film a documentary on a fashion show, the brainchild of Alphadi, a designer from Niger. Against the worst African odds he realised his dream of gathering top European and African designers for a fashion show in the desert. It was a surreal experience. Blue-robed Tuareg tribesmen, with their camels, sat in the dunes watching sexy models sashaying down a runway set in the sand. The logistics of feeding thousands of people were vast. Despite this, the food was surprisingly good. Cooked over open fires, the grilled *brochettes* were especially delicious. Here is my version.

Place the steak in a shallow dish. Put the onion, garlic, peanuts, chillies, ginger, salt and pepper in a food processor and pulse until roughly chopped. Add the oil and blitz until it forms a smooth paste. Spoon the marinade over the steak and toss thoroughly. Cover and refrigerate for 3 to 4 hours.

Thread the steak onto skewers, alternating with the onion chunks. Blitz the roasted peanuts and flour in a food processor in bursts until finely ground – don't overdo it or it will turn into peanut butter. Roll each kebab in the flour and peanut mixture until evenly coated. Cook over hot coals for 2 to 3 minutes per side for medium-rare.

V Vegetarian option: replace the steak with chunks of large black mushrooms.

- ¼ cup sesame oil
- 1 dry red chilli, chopped
- ½ cup raw peanuts
- 10 cloves garlic, peeled and bruised slightly
- 10 thick slices ginger
- 6 skinless chicken breast fillets, cut into bite-sized pieces
- ¼ cup soy sauce
- ¼ cup rice wine
- 2 teaspoons sugar
- 10 dried shiitake mushrooms, soaked, stems removed and caps sliced
- 4 spring onions, cut into 2 cm lengths
- squeeze of lemon
- fresh basil leaves

SERVES 6

Chinese 'no name' chicken with mushrooms and peanuts

In rural China, we became used to being stared at. As we went to areas where few foreigners had visited, we were a novelty. My red hair was especially alien. And the locals didn't just look and then glance away – they would stand and stare with open mouths.

Eating out became an adventure. Menus were useless as they were written in Chinese characters and nobody spoke English. Instead, we would walk around the restaurant until we saw someone eating something that looked good and order that. This recipe is one of those delicious 'no name' dishes.

Heat the sesame oil in a large, heavy pan and add the chilli and peanuts. Stir-fry for 2 to 3 minutes. Add the garlic and ginger, and stir-fry till fragrant. Add the chicken and stir-fry until it just changes colour.

Add the soy sauce, rice wine and sugar to the pan. Bring to the boil, stirring occasionally. Add the mushrooms and turn the heat down to low. (For more on shiitake, see page 90.) Cook uncovered for about 20 to 30 minutes, until the sauce reduces and thickens.

Add the spring onions and turn the heat back up to high. As soon as the sauce starts boiling, remove from the heat and add a squeeze of lemon and some basil leaves. Serve with jasmine rice.

V Vegetarian option: replace the chicken with extra shiitake mushrooms.

MARINADE

- 1 tablespoon tomato sauce
- 2 tablespoons sweet chilli
  sauce (see recipe page 94)
- 4 tablespoons Chinese plum
  sauce (see recipe page 42)
- 1 tablespoon rice
  wine vinegar
- 2 tablespoons finely grated
  ginger
- 1 tablespoon vodka
- 2 teaspoons red curry paste
  (see recipe page 227)
- ¼ cup water
- zest of a naartjie,
  plus juice

SOSATIES

- 750 g pork fillet, cubed
- peanut oil
- 2 or 3 naartjies, peeled and
  divided into segments
- 10 spring onions, cut into
  5 cm lengths
- 8 skewers – use fresh sticks
  of rosemary or bay for
  extra flavour

SAUCE

- ¼ cup naartjie juice
- 2 tablespoons butter

SERVES 4

Pork and naartjie sosaties

In the late 1980s I lived in an old farm house near Nasrec and Uncle Charlie's, south of Johannesburg. It was a tired old abode. At night it would creak and groan. If you turned on the toaster, the lights would dim. With its friendly wraparound veranda and sheltering oak trees, it had seen years of occupants leave their mark. One of the most memorable was the large slogan spray-painted on the front wall: *A Naartjie in our Sosatie* (Anarchy in our Society).

The house is long gone, replaced by rows of little suburban boxes. This recipe is in its memory.

MARINADE

Mix all the marinade ingredients together. Place the pork in a large shallow dish, add the marinade and mix well. Cover and leave in the fridge to marinate for 2 to 3 hours.

SOSATIES

Remove the pork from the fridge and drain, reserving the marinade. Thread the pork onto the skewers, alternating with naartjie segments and spring onions. Place on a rack over a roasting pan to catch the juice and grill for 6 to 8 minutes, turning and basting with the marinade, until the pork is cooked.

SAUCE

While the pork is cooking, pour a cup of the reserved marinade and the naartjie juice into a saucepan. Bring to the boil and let it simmer until reduced to about half a cup. When the pork is cooked, add any juices from the roasting pan to the sauce. Add the butter and stir through until melted. Drizzle the sauce over the sosaties and serve.

▼ Vegetarian option: replace the pork with chunks of bean curd puffs (squares of deep-fried tofu, which are super-absorbent and much chewier than plain tofu). You can find them in most Chinese supermarkets.

Caramel ginger tart

My mother is an avid recipe collector. In her kitchen is a lever-arch file bursting with handwritten recipes, which have been passed down from my grandmother and her grandmother before her. Then there are the recipes from friends and sisters, aunts and cousins, all scribbled on pieces of paper.

This habit runs in the family — my cousin Sue recently told me about an old family recipe book she has, which is jokingly called *To Destroy Tigers* as this is the last 'recipe' in the book.

She was paging through this tattered relic one day and out fell *Uncle Hammy's Recipe for Garlick Insecticide*. Our Great-Uncle Hammy lived on a farm outside Somerset West, drove tanks in the First World War and grew delicious organic grapes. Neither his Garlick Insecticide nor the tiger recipe is appropriate for this book. However, my ginger tart recipe, adapted from one handed down to me by my mother, is.

- 2 cups cake flour
- 2 tablespoons caster sugar
- ½ teaspoon ground ginger
- 150 g butter, cut into small cubes
- zest of 1 lime
- 1 or 2 tablespoons iced water

SHORTCRUST PASTRY

Sieve the flour, sugar and ginger into a bowl. Add the cubed butter and the lime zest and use your hands to quickly rub the butter and zest into the flour and sugar until it resembles fine breadcrumbs. Don't over mix it otherwise the butter will melt and the pastry will lose its flakiness.

Sprinkle a teaspoon or two of water over the top and, using a knife, cut and turn the mixture until it starts clumping together. Use your hands to bring the mixture together, adding water a little at a time until the bowl is clean of crumbs and the mixture is gathered into a ball. Place the ball between 2 sheets of plastic wrap and roll it evenly to fit a 22 cm tart dish. Remove from the plastic wrap and place in the dish. Leave it to rest in the fridge for at least half an hour and for up to 3 days.

Remove the pastry shell from the fridge, line it with greaseproof paper and sprinkle dried beans on top to hold it down. Bake at 180 °C for 15 to 20 minutes, until golden.

- 1½ tablespoons cornflour
- 3 ml ground ginger
- 1½ cups milk
- pinch salt
- ½ cup golden syrup
- ⅓ cup preserved ginger syrup
- 1½ cups water
- 1 egg, beaten
- ½ teaspoon butter
- 2 tablespoons chopped preserved ginger
- 150 ml cream, whipped
- extra preserved ginger for decoration

SERVES 8

FILLING

Mix the cornflour and ginger with a little of the milk until smooth. Heat the rest of the milk, salt, golden syrup, ginger syrup and water to boiling point. Whisk in the cornflour mixture, stir well and cook until thick. Slowly add the hot mixture to the beaten egg, stirring all the time. Tip the mixture back into the pot and heat until it just reaches boiling point. Remove from the heat and add the butter and preserved ginger. Pour the mixture into the prepared crust. Refrigerate until set. Top with whipped cream and preserved ginger. As an alternative, use the preserved ginger in lemon grass syrup on page 228.

HORSERADISH

My uncle grows horseradish on his farm in the Western Cape. When driving up the farm road, the pungent smell of horseradish in the air almost makes one's eyes water. Be warned, fresh horseradish is a demon when it comes to preparing it. The hot bite of a sauce made using fresh horseradish is completely different to the insipid flavour of most commercial preparations.

Harvesting, buying and storing horseradish

In late autumn lift several large roots – choose the thicker central ones rather than the rubbery side roots. When shopping for horseradish, look for larger stems rather than spindly ones. Choose ones that look firm and fresh. Older roots start shrivelling and look dry.

Store unwashed in a plastic bag in the fridge for up to a week. Once it is cut or grated, use it within a day or two. It can also be peeled, sliced and added to vodka. This will preserve it and create vodka with a horseradish kick that is fantastic in a Bloody Mary! Store your horseradish vodka in the freezer.

Horseradish is best preserved in vinegar. Wash the roots and trim off any green ends. Peel them under running water to prevent your eyes from tearing. Chop in a food processor until the horseradish is pulped. If necessary add a few teaspoons of water to help it along. Be careful – cut horseradish is far stronger than any onion, so keep your face away from the bowl. For every 3 tablespoons of grated horseradish, add 1 tablespoon of white wine vinegar, 1 teaspoon of sugar and a pinch of salt. Decant into sterilised bottles (see page 239), seal and store in the fridge for up to 6 months.

Salmon bombs with Bloody Mary granita

The best sushi I have ever eaten was in Long Beach, California. It was only a small fish restaurant, with wooden tables on a deck, where you could sit and watch the container ships coming into port. I first ate unagi, or eel rolls here.

Sushi is easy to make and it's not nearly as expensive as buying it at a restaurant. These salmon bombs are perfect as a starter or a party snack. They look as if they are just balls of rice – but waiting inside is an unexpected explosion of flavour. This is a fun take on sushi and you don't need any bamboo rolling mats or other paraphernalia.

- 3 cups short-grain sushi rice
- 3¼ cups water
- 4 tablespoons rice vinegar
- 1 tablespoon sugar
- 1 teaspoon salt

SALMON BOMBS
- 100g smoked salmon, cut into small pieces
- 1 large avocado, peeled and cut into small pieces
- 2 tablespoons wasabi mustard
- 4 tablespoons pickled ginger
- black sesame seeds
- sushi soy sauce for serving

MAKES APPROXIMATELY
30 BOMBS

RICE

The first step to successful sushi is making the rice properly. Rinse the rice until the water runs clear. Put the rice and water into a pot and bring to the boil over high heat. As soon as it is boiling hard, reduce heat to very low, cover and cook for about 20 minutes, until the water is almost all gone. Avoid opening the pot too often to check. Turn heat off and leave to steam on the stove for about 15 minutes.

While the rice is cooking, mix the rice vinegar, sugar and salt in a pan. Heat it gently until the sugar dissolves, remove from heat and cool.

Sprinkle the vinegar mixture over the rice and mix it in quickly with a wooden spatula. Tip the rice out onto a tray and spread it out. Fan it, using a paper plate or a fan, while you continue to turn it gently so that it cools evenly. Be careful not to mush it. Fanning the air until the rice cools makes it shiny and easier to work with.

SALMON BOMBS

Have a bowl of water standing by to keep your fingers wet, as it is much easier to work with sticky sushi rice using damp fingers. Place a small piece of salmon in your palm. Add a little avocado, a dab of wasabi and a small piece of pickled ginger. Take a spoonful of sushi rice and place it over the salmon mixture, covering it completely. Cover the rice with a piece of plastic wrap and turn it upside down, into the other palm. Press the rice up around the filling, adding more rice if needed, until the filling is completely encased. Twist the plastic wrap closed around the rice and shape it into a ball. Aim for a ball that is a perfect

mouthful, so don't make it too big. Untwist the plastic and place the ball on a tray. Repeat with the remaining rice and filling.

Once you have finished them all, sprinkle with the black sesame seeds, rolling them while you do it so that the bombs are coated evenly. Serve with a bowl of Bloody Mary granita and soy sauce for dipping.

BLOODY MARY GRANITA

Mix all the ingredients together and pour into a flat baking dish. Place it in the freezer and leave for about an hour. Remove and stir with a fork, fluffing up and aerating all the icy bits. Repeat this for the next 3 hours until all the liquid is frozen and fluffed. Leave it for a further 6 hours or overnight. Scrape out scoops of granita and serve with the salmon bombs.

BLOODY MARY GRANITA

- 2 cups tomato juice
- ¼ cup vodka
- 2 tablespoons finely chopped fresh horseradish
- ¼ teaspoon black pepper
- 1 teaspoon salt
- squeeze of lime juice

- ½ cup tomato sauce
- ¼ cup fresh horseradish (see page 141)
- Tabasco sauce to taste
- lemon juice to taste
- dozen oysters
- wedges of lemon

SERVES 2 AS A STARTER

Oysters with horseradish and tomato sauce

I ate my first oysters at the Acme Oyster House in New Orleans when I was 33. I had avoided them up until then. (Okay, I admit it, I was being a coward.) Keith ordered a platter of 12 oysters for $2.99 and I ordered my calamari. When his oysters arrived, he convinced me to try one with a dollop of spicy horseradish and tomato sauce. Within a few minutes, we had ordered a second platter of oysters with cold beer and saltine crackers. I was hooked.

As we travelled through the southern states, I hunted out the oyster bars and their 'happy hour' specials. I ate my way through dozens of oysters, from the first ones in New Orleans to Pappy and Jimmy's in Memphis. I have since eaten oysters many other ways, but none beat this first taste sensation.

Mix the first 4 ingredients together until smooth. Serve the oysters on a bed of crushed ice with the sauce in a dipping bowl and extra wedges of lemon on the side. (Saltine crackers and beer are optional.)

- 3 tablespoons finely chopped fresh horseradish
- 1 teaspoon Dijon mustard
- ¼ cup sour cream
- 1 tablespoon mayonnaise
- 1 tablespoon chopped chives

Horseradish sauce

Horseradish has a mighty bite – but it loses its strength very quickly. Most commercial horseradish sauce is a bland baby-food version of fresh homemade horseradish sauce. This sauce is delicious with roast beef and is also great added to a tartare sauce.

Mix all the ingredients together until smooth and store in an airtight container. This sauce will keep in the fridge for a few days.

LETTUCE AND SPINACH

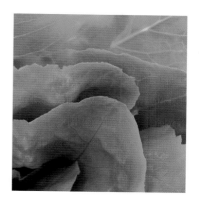

Both lettuce and spinach are stalwarts of my garden. With our climate we can grow them almost all year round. We can also grow a wider variety than we find on most supermarket shelves. A salad made from freshly picked baby spinach leaves, tossed with frilly, crunchy green and red lettuce leaves needs little more added to it.

Harvesting, buying and storing lettuce and spinach

Harvest by plucking single leaves off a few plants, rather than picking one whole plant. This will extend the harvest. Pick them either early in the morning or after sunset and dunk the leaves into a large basin of cold water to rinse off any dust. Spin them dry in small batches. Once you have torn up the leaves for a salad or chopped spinach for a stir-fry, spin them again to make sure they are completely dry. Salad dressing sticks better to dry leaves and dry greens stir-fry quicker – if they are wet, they tend to steam, not fry.

When buying spinach look for bunches with crisp, fresh leaves. Limp leaves are a no-no. Try to find a greengrocer who supplies a variety of whole lettuces rather than buying mixed leaves in a bag, unless you plan to eat them in one sitting. All greens are best eaten soon after picking, but if you do need to store them for a day or two, keep them as dry as possible by sealing them in a zip lock bag with paper towels (see page 239). If you have excess spinach, freezing works well, as long as it is prepared properly. (See Freezing vegetables on page 235.)

TUNA

- 5 tablespoons soy sauce
- 5 tablespoons sake
- 5 tablespoons mirin
- 800 g tuna, cut into bite-sized pieces
- 1 bowl of whole cos lettuce leaves

WASABI AVOCADO PEAR

- 2 avocado pears, halved, stoned and skinned
- 4 teaspoons sushi soy sauce
- 1½ teaspoons sesame oil
- 2 tablespoons rice vinegar
- 2 teaspoons wasabi paste
- 1 tablespoon black sesame seeds

SERVES 4

Teriyaki tuna and wasabi avocado pear wrapped in lettuce

This is a fresh way to serve a picnic lunch. Help yourself to a lettuce leaf 'bowl', fill it with a mouthful of fish, top it with some avocado and pop it into your mouth. No fuss, no mess – and no washing up. I love using a variety of greens as wraps for a filling. They are much lighter than using tortillas or pita bread. Baby cabbage, spinach and lettuce all work well.

TUNA

Whisk the soy sauce, sake and mirin together. Place the tuna in a dish and pour the marinade over. Cover and marinate in the fridge, stirring occasionally, for 4 to 5 hours.

Drain the fish and spread onto a baking tray. Grill for a few minutes, turning and basting with the marinade, until just cooked. Serve wrapped in the lettuce leaves, topped with some wasabi avocado.

WASABI AVOCADO PEAR

Cut the avocado pear into bite-sized pieces. Mix the remaining ingredients together until smooth. Just before serving, toss the avocado pear together with the dressing.

Quick chicken curry with spinach

- 4 tablespoons butter
- 2 onions, finely sliced
- 3 large cloves garlic, diced
- 2 stalks lemon grass, bruised
- 2 tablespoons ground coriander
- 1 tablespoon ground cumin
- ¼ teaspoon ground cloves
- ½ teaspoon chilli powder
- salt to taste
- 700 g skinless chicken breast fillets, cut into bite-sized pieces
- 1 x 400 ml can of coconut cream
- 1 bunch spinach, washed well and roughly chopped
- 1 large red mild chilli, deseeded and sliced into strips
- a squeeze of lime juice

SERVES 4

I don't know who coined the culinary phrase 'to sweat'. It means to cook in butter, slowly over low heat, usually covered, without browning. Couldn't they have come up with a tastier term to describe such a delicious way of cooking?

Onions love being cooked in butter — it draws out their caramelised sweetness. If you really don't want to use butter, use olive oil instead. This robustly spiced curry combines with the chicken and spinach to create a very fresh taste.

Heat the butter in a cast iron pot. Add the onions and cook over low heat for about 10 minutes until softened and just starting to turn golden. Add the garlic and cook, stirring occasionally, for about 2 minutes more.

Turn up the heat a little. Add the lemon grass, coriander, cumin, cloves, chilli and salt. Stir until fragrant. Add the chicken and cook until just starting to change colour. Add the coconut cream and bring to a simmer until thickened slightly.

Add the spinach to the curry sauce and stir through until just wilted. Add the chilli strips, remove from the stove and finish with a squeeze of lime. Serve with basmati rice and Sweet potato and habanero chutney (see page 226).

V Vegetarian option: increase the amount of spinach and add a can of rinsed and drained chickpeas when you add the coconut cream.

Arizona ostrich steak stuffed with spinach and peppadew

A vegetarian friend of mine, who grew up on a farm, swore she would never marry a farmer. She duly married a film producer. Years later, when we were travelling across the United States, we stayed with them in Arizona. Her producer husband had given up the film industry and followed the 'ostrich rush' to the USA. As a new industry, it promised big returns for those who could successfully raise breeding pairs of ostrich. And my hapless vegetarian friend found herself married to a farmer after all.

Ostrich steak is rich and tender. The sweet but peppery spinach stuffing complements it very well.

SPINACH AND PEPPADEW

- 50 g butter
- 1 red onion, thinly sliced
- 200 g spinach, washed and spun-dried
- 1 teaspoon fresh rosemary, chopped
- 2 tablespoons flour
- ½ cup milk
- ½ cup cream
- 10 bottled peppadews, sliced
- salt and pepper to taste

OSTRICH STEAK

- salt and coarse black pepper
- 750 g ostrich fillets
- olive oil
- 1 teaspoon butter
- 1 teaspoon flour
- ½ cup cream
- few sprigs rosemary
- ½ teaspoon sugar

SERVES 4

SPINACH AND PEPPADEW

Heat the butter in a large saucepan. Add the onion and sauté over medium heat until softened. Meanwhile, cut any thick stems out of the spinach and chop them finely. Roughly chop the spinach leaves. Add the stems and rosemary to the onion and sauté for about 2 minutes. Add the spinach leaves and sauté until completely softened and the colour has changed to dark green.

Sprinkle the flour into the pan, stirring to distribute it evenly. Cook for about 2 minutes, adding more butter if necessary. Remove from heat and slowly add the milk and cream, stirring constantly to prevent the flour from forming lumps. Return to the stove and bring to a simmer, stirring occasionally, until it thickens. Add the peppadews, and then the salt and pepper to taste. Set aside.

OSTRICH STEAK

Heat the oven to 200°C. Mix the salt and coarse pepper in a bowl, and pat both sides of the fillets with the mixture. Heat some olive oil in a cast iron frying pan until shimmering. Add the steaks and cook for 2 to 3 minutes per side.

Remove from heat and cut each fillet three-quarters of the way through, horizontally. Fill with the spinach mixture and place in an oven-proof dish. (Keep any leftover spinach warm for serving with the steak.) Cover the dish with aluminium foil and place in the oven. Cook for 8 to 10 minutes.

While the steaks are cooking, return the cast iron pan to the heat. Add the

butter and as it melts, stir the bottom of the pan, scraping up any bits of meat. Sprinkle with flour and mix it into the butter. Keep stirring until the flour is slightly brown. Remove from the heat and add the cream slowly, stirring all the time. Add the rosemary sprigs and return to the heat, add the sugar and bring to a simmer, stirring until the sauce thickens.

Serve the steaks drizzled with the cream sauce, with a little extra spinach and peppadew on the side.

POTATOES

The first time I harvested potatoes from my garden I wasn't even sure there would be any. The plants had grown healthily and had flowered, but until I dug, I didn't know whether there would actually be any fat potatoes underground. But there were – way more than I expected. The excitement as I uncovered one fat tuber after another took me back to being a child, hunting for Easter eggs.

In my small garden I can never grow enough potatoes to supply us all year round, especially as we eat a lot of them. They are incredibly versatile and are full of nutrients. I very seldom peel potatoes, not only because I like the taste of the skin but leaving it on helps retain the nutrients during cooking. The skin also contains loads of fibre.

Harvesting, buying and storing potatoes

Potatoes are ready to be harvested a few weeks after the top green growth has died back. Using a fork, dig as far under the plant as you can and lift the soil, shaking the earth loose from the potatoes. Be careful not to stick the fork into the potatoes. Baby potatoes can be harvested earlier; a few weeks after they have finished flowering, rummage around in the top layers of soil with your hands to find the new, small baby potatoes.

Freshly harvested potatoes are quite fragile and need to be left for a couple of weeks for their skins to harden. If the weather is dry, leave them on the ground but if it is raining, gently lift them and store them in a cool dark place for a few weeks. Potatoes need to be stored in the dark otherwise they will turn green. Exposure to natural or artificial light leads to a build up of solanine, a toxic, bitter-tasting alkaloid. Avoid buying potatoes with even a vaguely greenish tinge.

I store my potatoes in a strong brown paper bag on an under-counter veggie rack. I mix up leaves of mint, rosemary, lavender and sage and place them at the bottom of the bag. The volatile oils help prevent decomposition and also prevent the potatoes from sprouting.

Flamenco chorizo and potato salad

One night in Seville, we went to watch flamenco dancing. It was a memorable performance – sultry, passionate and transporting. It is a tradition in Spain, when attending a really good performance, to call out *'Agua! Agua!'* – meaning the performance is so hot the dancers need to be doused with 'Water! Water!' Afterwards we went to a little tapas bar around the corner and filled up on great Spanish food. This dish brings back the memories.

- 2 large potatoes
- olive oil
- salt to taste
- 1 tablespoon fresh rosemary
- 10 cm piece of chilli chorizo
- 12 mini corn cobs, sliced
- 1 can chickpeas, rinsed
- 1 cup seedless grapes
- ½ cup red cherry tomatoes
- 1 wheel feta

- ¼ cup each of chopped parsley and mint
- 2 tablespoons whole-grain mustard
- 1 tablespoon balsamic vinegar
- 3 tablespoons olive oil
- salt and pepper to taste

SERVES 6 AS A SIDE DISH OR
A STARTER

SALAD

Heat the oven to 200°C. Cut the potatoes into small pieces and toss with some olive oil, salt and chopped rosemary. Spread out on a baking tray and roast for 30 to 45 minutes, until cooked.

Slice the chorizo, then cut into quarters. Heat some more olive oil in a cast iron frying pan and fry the chorizo until crispy. Add the corn and cook until just browned. Remove from the pan and leave to cool a little.

Mix the roasted potatoes, chorizo and corn with the chickpeas, grapes and tomatoes in a serving bowl, and toss with the dressing. Crumble the feta over the top and serve.

DRESSING

To make the dressing, mix all the ingredients together well and toss with the salad.

V Vegetarian option: instead of chorizo, add half a cup of raw cashew nuts to the oil and cook, stirring, until browned.

APPLE AND SAGE SAUCE

- 4 apples
- 3 tablespoons salted butter
- 2 tablespoons brown sugar
- 10 fresh sage leaves

PORK CHOPS

- 3 tablespoons Thai sweet
  chilli sauce (see page 94)
- 1 tablespoon ketjap manis
  (see page 250)
- 1½ teaspoons sesame oil
- 6 boneless pork chops

POTATOES

- 20 baby potatoes, halved
- olive oil
- 3 garlic cloves, diced
- ½ cup parsley, chopped
- ¼ cup chives, chopped
- sea salt to taste
- squeeze of lime juice

SERVES 6

Glazed pork chops with apple and sage sauce and crispy garlic potatoes

My late mother-in-law, Wendy, made the greatest roast potatoes. With their thick crunchy exterior and moist, fleshy centre, they were always snapped up at family lunches. These crispy potatoes are inspired by the memory of her wonderful recipe.

For the pork chops I have mixed and matched flavours a little bit by combining classic English accompaniments (apple and sage) with some Asian ingredients in the glaze. I love the combination of salty and sweet, which works particularly well with pork.

APPLE AND SAGE SAUCE

Peel and core the apples, and cut into pieces. Place the slices in a baking dish, dot with butter and sprinkle with sugar. Scatter with the sage leaves and bake for 45 minutes at 200°C, stirring occasionally. Remove from the oven and leave to cool a little. Blitz in a food processor until smooth. Add 2 teaspoons of the pork glaze (see below) and mix through.

PORK CHOPS

Mix the first 3 ingredients together for the glaze, keeping 2 teaspoons aside for the apple sauce. Grill the pork chops for about 4 minutes a side. Brush with glaze and grill for a further 1 to 2 minutes. Serve with the apple and sage sauce and crispy garlic potatoes.

POTATOES

Steam or microwave the potatoes until just tender. Heat some olive oil in a cast iron pan. Dry the potatoes well and toss them into the pan. Cook over medium heat, turning occasionally, until evenly golden and crisp, about 20 minutes to half an hour. About 5 minutes before serving, add the garlic (if necessary add some more oil). Remove from heat, sprinkle with parsley, chives and salt, and add a squeeze of lime. Serve immediately.

- 1 kg potatoes
- 1 tablespoon powdered wasabi
- ½ cup cream
- ½ cup milk
- 6 tablespoons butter
- salt and pepper, to taste

SERVES 6 AS A SIDE DISH

Wasabi mashed potatoes

These mashed potatoes are given an extra zing with the addition of wasabi. Try them with pork sausages for bangers and mash with a difference.

I like finding chunks of potato skin in my mash, but if you prefer a really smooth mashed potato then peel your potatoes first.

Quarter the potatoes and steam them until just tender. Mix the wasabi, cream and milk together in a saucepan. Warm through over a low heat. Mash the potatoes using a potato masher, and add the butter, and warm cream and milk mixture. Mash until smooth. Do not over-mash otherwise they will become gluey. Season with salt and pepper to taste.

RIBS
- 2 kg rack of pork ribs, cut in half across the middle
- ½ cup tomato sauce
- ½ cup Thai sweet chilli sauce (see page 94)
- 1 teaspoon brown sugar
- 2 tablespoons Worcestershire sauce
- 1 teaspoon lemon juice
- 1 tablespoon French mustard
- 2 tablespoons light soy sauce
- ½ cup red wine
- 1 cup water

SERVES 4

'White Trash' pork ribs with sesame potatoes

I was browsing through a bookstore in California when I stumbled across a cookbook called *White Trash Cooking*. The very first recipe in the book was *Uncle Willie's Swamp Cabbage Stew*. This temptation was followed by other gems such as *Mama Leila's Hand-Me-Down Oven-Baked Possum* and *Kiss Me Not Sandwiches*. I had to have this book!

I then discovered its sequel, *White Trash Cooking II: Recipes for Gatherin's*. The following recipe was inspired by *Uncle Bubba's Barbecued Ribs*. The best!

RIBS

Heat oven to 160°C. Place the ribs on a baking tray. Mix the remaining ingredients together and pour over the ribs. Place in the oven and bake, turning and basting every 20 minutes, for an hour.

Remove from the oven and drain off excess marinade, reserving it to baste. Return ribs to the oven and continue cooking and basting for a further hour. Just before serving, brown under the grill for 2 to 3 minutes per side.

SESAME POTATOES

These potatoes can be served either hot or cold. If serving cold, use olive oil instead of melted butter. Try an alternative version by substituting a sprinkling of fried Chinese garlic (see page 29) for the sesame seeds.

Steam, boil or microwave the potatoes until just cooked. While they are cooking, heat the butter in a small saucepan until melted. Add the lemon juice and sesame seeds, stir through and remove from heat. Place the potatoes in a bowl and toss with the lemon butter and parsley. Sprinkle with sea salt to taste.

- 5 large potatoes, cut into quarters
- 1 tablespoon butter
- 1 teaspoon lemon juice
- 2 tablespoons black sesame seeds
- 1 teaspoon parsley, finely chopped
- sea salt to taste

ROCKET

Rocket is one of my favourite greens. It grows like a weed, it flourishes all year round and it is delicious. What's not to like? It is also versatile and can be eaten raw or cooked. Also known by its Italian name – *arugula* – it has a distinctive peppery, mustardy flavour. I grow a few different varieties of rocket. Some have wide leaves with white flowers and a mild flavour. Others have skinny leaves, yellow flowers and are far more pungent. If you leave the plants to go to seed, you will have rocket year round in your garden.

Harvesting, buying and storing rocket

Harvest single leaves from a few bushes. Younger leaves are more tender and their flavour is not as strong. Older leaves are tougher and more pungent, and these are the ones I cook.

At the market, look for crisp fresh leaves – ignore the wilted ones. Rocket is at its best soon after picking. If you have to store it, don't wash it first. (See page 239 for ideas on how best to store greens.) Rocket will keep only for a day or two at the most. It can easily be made into pesto. Follow the recipe on page 70, using rocket instead of basil.

RIBS

- 2 large garlic cloves, finely diced
- 2 tablespoons ginger, finely sliced
- ½ cup dark soy sauce
- 3 tablespoons dark brown sugar
- ½ cup water
- ⅓ cup sake or Chinese wine
- 1 teaspoon ground hot red chilli, or to taste
- 1 teaspoon five-spice powder
- 2 tablespoons lime juice
- 1 kg beef short ribs

SERVES 6

Sticky ribs with rice and Asian soup

We spent a couple of months travelling through China and wherever we went we would invariably find some hawker or little noodle stall selling bowls of steaming hot, meaty broth. Served with fresh vegetables, noodles and crispy barbecued meat, it soon became a favourite and filling meal.

Here is my version. Rocket adds a fresh peppery crunch to this delicious soup. It is worth making a batch of Chinese beef stock (see page 232) and freezing it.

RIBS

Combine all the ingredients (except the ribs) in a saucepan and cook over medium heat until the sugar has dissolved. Place the ribs in a shallow oven-proof dish and pour the marinade over them. Cover and marinate for 3 to 4 hours.

Heat the oven to 160°C. Pour off a third of a cup of marinade for the soup. Cover the ribs with aluminium foil or a lid and bake for 2 hours. Remove the aluminium foil and cook for a further hour, basting and turning occasionally.

SOUP

Heat the peanut oil in a large wok until shimmering. Add the garlic and stir-fry for 15 seconds. Add the ginger and chilli, and stir-fry for a further 30 seconds. Add the stock and apple juice and bring to the boil. Add the reserved beef rib marinade and simmer for about 2 minutes.

Roughly chop the broccoli and just before serving add it and the snow peas to the broth. Simmer until just wilted. Remove from the heat, stir the rocket into

SOUP

- peanut oil
- 2 large cloves garlic, finely diced
- ½ cm ginger root, peeled and finely diced
- 1 small dried red chilli, chopped
- 1 litre Chinese beef stock (see page 231)
- ⅓ cup pure apple juice
- ⅓ cup reserved marinade
- 250 g tender stem broccoli
- 30 snow peas
- 2 cups fresh rocket
- lime juice, sugar and salt to taste
- egg noodles

SERVES 6

the soup, add a squeeze of lime juice, sugar and salt to taste. Serve in large bowls with egg noodles, topped with the ribs.

V Vegetarian option: replace the beef stock with vegetable stock. Instead of the ribs, marinade thick slices of eggplant, before roasting them until cooked.

HERB SALSA

- 5 nasturtium flowers
- 5 nasturtium leaves
- 10 green nasturtium seeds
- 2 fresh chillies
- 1 cup chopped coriander
- ¼ cup fresh basil, sliced
- 1 cup wild rocket, sliced
- 5 tomatoes, diced
- juice of a lime
- 1 tablespoon fried garlic
  (see page 29)
- 3 spring onions, sliced
- salt, sugar and pepper
- 1 avocado pear, cubed

REFRIED BEANS

- 1 packet streaky bacon
- 1 x 450 ml can red kidney
  beans

TOSTADA

- 4 flour tortillas
- 450 ml Mexican tomatoes
- ½ cup grated cheddar
- ½ cup grated mozzarella
- 1 cup sour cream
- sliced pickled jalapenos
- bowl of lettuce
- fresh coriander

SERVES 4

Mexican tostada with herb salsa and refried beans

A friend of mine who became a vegetarian says the thing he misses most about not eating meat is bacon. I can understand that. Bacon is so much more than breakfast. It is a quick and easy way to add flavour to many a meal. Its salty flavour is a perfect counterfoil for this verdant herb salsa.

Rocket and nasturtiums are ideal salad-bowl mates as they are peppery, fresh and crunchy.

HERB SALSA

Slice the nasturtium flowers, leaves and seeds, and put them in a medium-sized bowl. Chop the fresh chillies finely and add them to the bowl. Add the coriander, basil and rocket, and stir in the tomatoes and lime juice. Leave to mellow for a couple of hours.

Just before serving, mix in the garlic and spring onion, and add salt, sugar and pepper to taste. Gently toss the avocado pear into the salsa.

REFRIED BEANS

Fry the bacon in a pan until crisp. Drain on paper towels and set aside to use in the tostadas, leaving the bacon fat in the pan. Drain and rinse the kidney beans well and add them to the pan. Cook for about 5 minutes until softened. Tip into a bowl and mash until smooth. Set aside and keep warm.

TOSTADA

Heat the flour tortillas in a dry frying pan until warmed and softened. Place on a board and spread Mexican tomatoes (see page 226) evenly onto each one. Cut the bacon into bite-sized pieces and sprinkle on top. Mix the cheeses together and scatter over the bacon. Place under the grill until the cheese melts and starts to brown. Top with the herb salsa and serve with some sour cream, sliced jalapenos, lettuce, coriander and refried beans.

V Vegetarian option: use olive oil to cook the beans instead of bacon. Top the tostada with whole red kidney beans.

- 1 large colander rocket, washed and spun dry
- 2 cups olive oil
- 2 teaspoons salt
- 1 teaspoon black pepper

Rocket preserved in oil

As with basil, for longer storage, rather preserve your rocket in oil. This oil is great in pasta dishes and in a salad dressing.

Blend all the ingredients until smooth. Spoon into a sterilised jar (see page 239) and cover with olive oil. Seal and store in the fridge. Whenever you use it, make sure the top is covered with oil and it will keep for quite some time.

SALAD
- 1 bowl lettuce and rocket
- 10 ripe figs, cut into quarters
- 1 avocado pear, sliced
- ½ cup Gorgonzola cheese
- ½ cup walnuts, roasted

DRESSING
- ¼ cup plain yoghurt
- ¼ cup mayonnaise
- ¼ cup milk
- 1 teaspoon chilli jelly (see page 92)
- ¼ teaspoon freshly ground black pepper
- 1 tablespoon chopped fresh chives
- salt to taste

SERVES 4

Fig and walnut salad

Below the tennis court on my grandfather's farm was the orchard, filled with fruit and nut trees. During a tennis game, if a ball went over the back, an impromptu break would follow; the game put on hold while we stuffed our faces with ripe figs.

One year, when I was about seven or so, I was in the orchard. Too little to reach the ripe walnuts in the tree, I was picking ones that had fallen on the ground. My jeans pockets were full when I felt the first sting in the middle of my back.

The walnuts were riddled with red ants and they had stealthily crept all over me. As if the first ant had given a signal, they all started biting me at once. I am still wary of ants to this day but thank goodness the experience did not put me off walnuts.

I am lucky enough to have a walnut tree in my Johannesburg garden. Every year we harvest a huge basketful of walnuts, which I shell and freeze. Figs, Gorgonzola and walnuts are perfect companions.

To make the salad, place the lettuce and rocket on a serving platter. Toss the figs and avocado pear evenly on the bed of leaves. Crumble the cheese over the top and sprinkle with walnuts.

To make the dressing, whisk all the ingredients together until smooth. Just before serving, drizzle over the salad.

SWEET POTATOES

Sweet potatoes are truly meant for cold weather. There is something very heartening about sipping glühwein in front of a fire, while foil-wrapped bundles of red bliss bake on the hearth. They live up to the 'sweet' in their name and are a perfect foil for spicy, crunchy and fresh flavours. As with ordinary potatoes, they can be cooked in a variety of ways. My favourite is baked or roasted.

Harvesting, buying and storing sweet potatoes

Unearthing fat, pink sweet potato tubers means autumn is here. Harvest them before the frost hits and handle them gently. Leave them to dry for about three hours before bringing them inside to a well-ventilated, dark spot to sit for a week or so till the skins harden.

Buy sweet potatoes with as few blemishes as possible and look for ones that are heavy for their size. Sweet potatoes should be stored in a cool, dark, well-ventilated area.

- 2 tablespoons chopped fresh rosemary
- 1 tablespoon each fresh thyme, oregano and marjoram leaves, chopped
- 5 cloves garlic, roughly chopped
- 1 teaspoon salt
- ¼ teaspoon black pepper
- olive oil
- 750 g lamb knuckles
- 1 large onion, thickly sliced
- 2 parsnips, thickly sliced
- 2 carrots, thickly sliced
- 2 potatoes, cut into chunks
- 1 sweet potato, cut into chunks
- ½ cup red wine
- ½ cup orange juice
- 1½ cups water or beef stock (see page 231)
- 2 tablespoons tomato paste
- 2 tablespoons lemon zest
- 1 teaspoon cinnamon
- 1 tablespoon cumin
- ¼ teaspoon ground ginger
- 50 g pitted dates, chopped
- salt and pepper to taste

SERVES 4

Lamb tagine with fresh herbs and vegetables

I was given a tagine by the incredibly talented master potter Ian Glenny, one of the founders of the Midlands Meander. My tagine is beautiful, practical and huge – it only just fits into my oven. With autumn nights growing longer and colder, it is time to turn to slow-cooked dishes, perfect for my tagine. If you don't have one, use a cast iron pot instead.

Mix the herbs, garlic, salt and black pepper with some olive oil in a pestle and mortar. Pound until it forms a chunky paste. Rub the mixture over the lamb. Leave to rest while you peel and slice the veggies.

Heat the oven to 180 °C. Place the vegetables in an even layer on the bottom of the tagine. Add the lamb on top. Mix the red wine, orange juice, water (or beef stock), tomato paste, lemon zest, cinnamon, cumin, ginger and dates together and pour over the top. Cover and cook for 1 hour and then give it a stir. Turn the heat down to 160 °C and cook for a further 2 hours, until the meat is nearly falling off the bone. Taste and add salt and pepper.

Serve with fresh crusty bread.

V Vegetarian option: mix the herb paste with the vegetables, adding some chunks of butternut, and place in the tagine. Add rest of the ingredients, using vegetable stock instead of beef. Cook for an hour and then add slices of eggplant and a can of chickpeas, rinsed and drained. Cook for a further hour, until the vegetables are tender.

SWEET POTATOES AND CORIANDER CREAM CHEESE

- 4 sweet potatoes
- I cup smooth cream cheese
- ½ cup coriander leaves, finely chopped

RED CABBAGE SALAD WITH ROAST WALNUTS

- I tablespoon ketjap manis (see page 250)
- ½ teaspoon chilli powder
- ½ teaspoon sugar
- I teaspoon sesame oil
- ½ cup walnuts
- I red baby cabbage, finely sliced
- 20 red baby tomatoes, sliced in half
- I avocado pear, chopped
- 3 tablespoons walnut oil
- I tablespoon balsamic vinegar
- salt and pepper to taste
- ½ cup coriander leaves

SERVES 4

Baked sweet potatoes and coriander cream cheese, with red cabbage salad and roast walnuts

The first time I ate organic, home-grown sweet potatoes was on a farm near George. Freshly harvested that afternoon, we ate them at Leila's Arms, a restaurant that is part of Leila's Permaculture Estate. Leila's was a delight to visit. This family is not just talking about sustainability – they are living it. The buildings are made from local materials using straw bale techniques, the sun's energy is used for heating and cooking, and almost all their food comes from their own doorstep. Oh – and the sweet potatoes are legendary. This recipe is inspired by Leila's.

SWEET POTATOES AND CORIANDER CREAM CHEESE

Heat the oven to 180°C. Wrap the sweet potatoes in foil and bake for 45 minutes to an hour, until cooked through. Mix the cream cheese and coriander together and refrigerate while the potatoes cook. When the potatoes are done, split them open and dollop some cream cheese in the middle.

RED CABBAGE SALAD WITH ROAST WALNUTS

Mix the ketjap manis, chilli, sugar and sesame oil together, stirring until well mixed. (Some brands of ketjap manis are thicker than others. If it is too thick, add water to thin it out.) Add the walnuts and toss to coat. Pour the mixture through a strainer and drain the liquid.

Spread the walnuts onto a baking sheet and bake in the same oven with the potatoes, for about 10 minutes, turning occasionally. (These are delicious eaten on their own as a snack – try making them using a mixture of different nuts and seeds.)

Mix the cabbage, tomatoes and avocado pear together in a bowl. Whisk the oil and balsamic together and add salt and pepper to taste. Toss the dressing with the salad and sprinkle the baked walnuts and fresh coriander leaves on top. Serve with the sweet potatoes.

- 4 large sweet potatoes
- olive oil
- 1 teaspoon salt
- 2 teaspoons turmeric
- 700 g pork fillet, cut into bite-sized pieces
- 2 teaspoons peanut oil
- 1 teaspoon sesame oil
- 1 medium onion, diced finely
- 3 cloves garlic, diced
- 3 cm fresh ginger, grated
- 3 small red chillies, diced finely
- 1 teaspoon shrimp paste
- 1 x 400 ml can coconut milk
- 4 tomatoes, chopped
- 1 tablespoon fish sauce
- 1 stalk fresh lemon grass, finely chopped
- pinch or 2 of sugar
- 5 spring onions, cut into 5 cm lengths
- juice of ½ lime
- ½ cup coriander leaves, to serve

SERVES 4

Burmese red pork with roast sweet potato

The Burmese teashop is a national institution. On the side of any street, at all times of day or evening, men and women sit on tiny stools, clustered around low tables, sipping sweet strong tea or coffee. Everybody frequents them, from scholars to street sweepers. Beverages are accompanied by snacks, which reflect the strong Indian, Chinese and Thai influences on the local cuisine: samoosas, lemon grass curries, noodle salads and deep-fried pastries.

This warming pork curry reflects the Thai and Indian influences, with the Burmese twist of plenty of shrimp paste. The caramelised flavour of the roast sweet potato provides a perfect balance to the heat.

Preheat the oven to 200°C. Cut the sweet potatoes in thick slices and toss with olive oil. Place in an even layer in a roasting pan and cook for 20 to 30 minutes, until soft, turning half way through.

Mix the salt and turmeric together and rub it into the pork with your fingers. Leave to infuse for half an hour.

Heat the peanut and sesame oil in a pan and cook the onion for 5 to 8 minutes, until softened. Add the garlic, ginger, chilli and shrimp paste, and stir for a few minutes over medium heat until fragrant.

Add the pork and cook until it starts changing colour. Add the coconut milk and bring to the boil. Cook, stirring occasionally, for 3 to 5 minutes. Add the tomatoes, fish sauce, lemon grass and sugar and bring back to the boil. Reduce heat and simmer, uncovered, for 10 minutes. Add the spring onions and simmer for another minute or so. Remove from heat and add the lime juice.

To serve, place a few slices of roast sweet potato on a plate and top with the pork curry. Sprinkle with coriander leaves.

V Vegetarian option: replace the pork with chunks of firm tofu or bean curd puffs (see page 136). Instead of shrimp paste, use tamarind liquid and replace the fish sauce with soy sauce.

June 22 – September 21

In seed time learn, in harvest teach, in winter enjoy.
William Blake

For years I grew only herbs and greens in my vegetable garden during winter. Summer veggies seemed more fun and winter became a time of dormancy for my garden and for me. That all changed after I planted broccoli for the first time. It grew quickly into a luscious bed of edible heads. But the best surprise was how long they lasted. As long as I kept snipping off the newly developed side shoots before they flowered, we ate nutritious broccoli for months. Since then I have become far more active in my garden in winter and I am rewarded with an endless supply of delicious winter vegetables.

In season in winter

Asian greens	Cornflower	Rocket
Broccoli	Dried beans	Spinach
Brussels sprouts	Kale	Swiss chard
Cabbage	Mustard greens	Winter squash
Calendula	Pansies	
Cauliflower	Peas	

WINTER

Asian Greens

I always, no matter what time of year, have some kind of Asian greens growing in my garden. Most of these are cooler-season crops, going to seed quickly in the mid-summer heat. If you time your successive planting right, you will always have a fresh supply.

Piquant, peppery Asian greens include bok choy, tatsoi, pak choi, mizuna, Chinese cabbage, chrysanthemum greens, and green and red mustard. Baby leaves are a nutritious addition to salads and larger leaves can be stir-fried or added to soups.

Harvesting, buying and storing Asian greens

Harvest early in the morning before the day's heat has wilted them. To prolong a plant's life, pick from several plants rather than denuding one.

The best place to buy Asian greens is – surprise – an Asian supermarket. At Johannesburg's Chinatown in Cyrildene, a wide variety of freshly harvested greens are on sale daily. Choose the freshest ones and leave any that look limp or wilted. Asian greens are best eaten as soon after picking as possible. If you have to store them, place them in a zip lock bag with air added (see page 239) and keep them in the fridge for 2 to 3 days.

Asian noodle soup

This is my comfort food. We spent nine months travelling in Southeast Asia and in every country we visited there was some version of the ubiquitous noodle soup. It is surprisingly easy to make and the trick to creating a really yummy noodle soup is using a good-quality chicken stock (see page 232).

Cook the noodles in boiling water according to the instructions on the packet. Keep warm in a covered colander set over just-simmering water.

Heat the oil in a wok until shimmering. Add the garlic and stir-fry for 30 seconds. Add the ginger and chilli, stir-frying for a further 30 seconds. Add the chicken pieces and stir-fry until they change colour. Then add the 3 sauces, stirring well to mix. Add the chicken stock, cover and bring to the boil.

Add the Asian greens and simmer uncovered for 2 to 3 minutes. Just before serving, add the lime juice. Taste and add salt if required.

Place the reserved noodles in individual serving bowls and ladle the soup over, making sure that each bowl has some chicken and greens. Sprinkle with chopped coriander.

V Vegetarian option: replace the chicken stock with vegetable stock and the fish sauce with extra soy sauce. Instead of chicken, use a couple of carrots and daikon (Asian radish), sliced very thinly.

- 2 'nests' dried egg noodles
- 1 tablespoon peanut oil
- 2 cloves garlic, diced
- 1 tablespoon fresh ginger, finely chopped
- 1 fresh red chilli, finely chopped
- 2 skinless chicken breasts, sliced into bite-sized pieces
- 1 tablespoon dark soy sauce
- 1 tablespoon sweet chilli sauce
- 2 teaspoons fish sauce
- 1 litre chicken stock
- small bowl roughly chopped Asian greens
- juice of ¼ lime
- fresh coriander

SERVES 4 AS A STARTER

CHICKEN

- olive oil
- 4 chicken drumsticks
- 4 chicken breasts
- 1 teaspoon citrus and herb spice rub (see page 230)

DIPPING SAUCE

- 2 tablespoons sugar
- ½ cup water
- 2 teaspoons cornflour
- 2 tablespoons soy sauce
- 1 tablespoon rice vinegar
- 1 clove garlic, diced
- ½ teaspoon dried chilli flakes
- ½ teaspoon salt
- zest of a lemon

BOK CHOY

- 4 large whole bok choy
- peanut oil
- 3 cloves garlic, diced
- 3 tablespoons teriyaki sauce
- 1 large chunk tofu, drained and cubed
- sesame oil
- Japanese chilli (see page 250)
- Egg noodles, cooked

SERVES 4

Filipino crispy chicken with bok choy

When the millennium arrived we were island hopping in the Philippines. One common thread throughout was the Filipino love of a good barbecue. From the street-side vendors with small grills, to massive pavilions seating hundreds, we found superb grilled food everywhere.

Chicken heads, known colloquially as 'helmets' and the three-toed chicken legs, nicknamed 'Adidas' – not because they can run fast but because of their resemblance to the logo – are all on offer. After diners select their cut, it is grilled in front of them and the still-sizzling skewer is dipped into a sweet and sour sauce. The result? Succulent chicken, with crispy skin and tasty meat – just the way it should be.

CHICKEN

Preheat the oven to 220°C. Rub the olive oil over the chicken pieces, and rub the citrus and herb spice evenly over the skin. Place in one layer in a large baking tray, skin side up, and bake for 25 minutes. While the chicken is cooking, prepare the dipping sauce.

Turn the chicken over and bake for a further 15 minutes. Then turn back to skin-side up and grill for 3 to 4 minutes until the skin is crisp and browned.

DIPPING SAUCE

Bring the sugar and water to the boil in a small saucepan, stirring until the sugar is melted. Add a teaspoon or two of cold water to the cornflour. Mix it into a paste and then slowly stir it back into the sugar water. Add the soy sauce, vinegar, garlic, chilli, salt and lemon zest. Bring to the boil, stirring until it thickens.

BOK CHOY

Just before the chicken is ready to serve, stir-fry the bok choy. Cut the bottom off the bok choy and break into separate leaves. Wash well and spin dry. Heat the oil in the wok and add the garlic. Stir-fry for 15 seconds then add the bok choy. Stir-fry for a minute or two until just wilted. Add the teriyaki sauce and tofu, and stir-fry until heated through.

Remove from heat and sprinkle with sesame oil and chilli to taste. Spoon over some egg noodles. Serve the chicken with bok choy and bowls of dipping sauce on the side.

V Vegetarian option: this dish is perfect to serve at a dinner with both vegetarian and non-vegetarian guests. Make a larger portion of the bok choy and serve it in a separate bowl.

BROCCOLI

Broccoli plays many roles in the kitchen and it is not too fussy about its climate in the garden. Broccoli is surprisingly easy to grow and it continues producing side sprouts long after the central bud has been harvested. Whether eaten raw, lightly steamed or roasted, broccoli is extremely nutritious and delicious.

Harvesting, buying and storing broccoli

Harvest broccoli when the central bud is full but still compact. Cut it about 10 cm below the bud. It will continue to produce side shoots for a month or two, as long as you keep harvesting them and don't let them flower. When buying broccoli look for ones that are firm and uniformly green without any yellowing. Broccoli will keep for about a week in the fridge. Store it in a plastic bag. It also freezes well (see page 235).

Frittata with broccoli and cheese

One of the few dishes I could make as a teenager was a frittata. I didn't know then that it was called a frittata, but I loved making a dish that was a meal on its own. The trick to making it deliciously fluffy is to beat the egg whites before mixing them into the yolks.

Heat the oven to 180°C. Separate the egg yolks from the whites. Using a fork, beat the yolks with the chives, parsley, milk, salt and pepper until smooth. Whisk the whites until just fluffy – don't over whisk them, otherwise the frittata becomes too puffy.

Heat the butter in a large pan over medium heat. Add the yolks to the whites and gently fold them together until mixed. Swirl the butter in the pan so that it coats the bottom evenly and immediately pour in the egg mixture. Once the egg has started setting, after about 3 to 5 minutes, add the broccoli, ham and tomatoes, scattering them evenly on top of the egg. (They will sink a little into the top section of the egg, which should still be fluffy and uncooked. Don't worry – it will set in the oven.) Mix the 3 cheeses together and sprinkle them over the top.

If necessary, wrap some aluminium foil around the handle of the pan to protect it, and put it in the oven. Bake for 10 to 12 minutes, until the egg is set and the cheese is just starting to brown.

V Vegetarian option: replace the ham with sliced mushrooms.

- 4 eggs
- 1 teaspoon chopped chives
- 2 tablespoons chopped parsley
- 4 tablespoons milk
- salt and pepper to taste
- 1 tablespoon butter
- 1 cup broccoli florets, steamed
- ¼ cup diced ham
- ¼ cup tomatoes, sliced
- 3 tablespoons feta, crumbled
- 3 tablespoons cheddar, grated
- 2 tablespoons Parmesan, finely grated

SERVES 4

- 3 cups penne pasta
- 2 large heads broccoli
- 100 g smoked salmon, sliced
- 2 tablespoons capers
- 3 tomatoes, sliced
- salt and pepper to taste
- 4 tablespoons butter
- 3 cloves garlic, diced
- 1 teaspoon hot Spanish paprika
- 1 tablespoon dried oregano
- 4 tablespoons flour
- 800 ml milk
- ½ cup Parmesan, finely grated
- ¼ cup cheddar, grated
- extra grated Parmesan and mozzarella
- breadcrumbs

SERVES 4

Smoked salmon and broccoli baked pasta

If you are not a fan of baked pasta dishes because they are too dense and heavy with soggy pasta and gluey sauce, try this recipe. The secret to making baked pasta with a light interior and crispy crust is to cook it at a high temperature. As the pasta is already almost cooked, you don't want it slow cooking and soaking up the moisture from the sauce – and becoming soggy in the process. Use a large shallow dish rather than a deep one as this maximises the surface area and increases the amount of yummy crust.

Heat the oven to 210°C. Cook the penne till *al dente* and drain. Cut the broccoli into florets and steam until just tender. Toss the broccoli, salmon, capers and pasta together in an oven-proof dish. Lay the sliced tomatoes on top. Sprinkle with some salt and black pepper to taste.

Heat the butter in a large saucepan. Add the garlic and sauté until softened. Add the paprika and oregano and cook for a further 1 to 2 minutes. Add the flour and stir occasionally for 2 to 3 minutes. Remove from the heat and add the milk slowly, stirring constantly so the flour does not form lumps. Return to the stove and stir regularly, until the sauce comes to the boil and thickens. Add the Parmesan and cheddar cheese and stir through until melted. Add salt and pepper to taste.

Pour the sauce over the penne, vegetables and salmon in the baking dish. Cover the top with a layer of mixed Parmesan and mozzarella, and sprinkle with breadcrumbs. Bake uncovered, for 10 to 15 minutes, until the top is browned and the sauce bubbling.

V Vegetarian option: replace the salmon with thinly sliced strips of carrot, steamed until just cooked.

CRÊPES

- 1 teaspoon oil
- 1 egg
- 1 cup milk
- 1 cup flour
- pinch of salt

FILLING

- 2 tablespoons butter
- 2 tablespoons flour
- 1 cup milk
- 1 teaspoon paprika
- ½ teaspoon salt
- 2 tablespoons cream cheese
- ¼ cup vodka
- 100 g smoked salmon, sliced
- 100 g broccoli florets, steamed
- 2 tablespoons chives, chopped
- 2 tablespoons green nasturtium seeds, chopped
- black pepper to taste
- handful nasturtium flowers for garnishing

SERVES 2 AS A MAIN COURSE, OR 4 AS A STARTER

Icelandic crêpes with nasturtiums, vodka and salmon

We spent a week in Iceland once, visiting a friend who married an Icelandic man, whose name I cannot pronounce. It is a country of fascinating contrasts; raw and volcanic with steaming hot lakes of ice-blue water, sulphurous geothermal heating and frozen waterfalls. A country of fire and ice. Iceland's vodka, called Reyka, after the Icelandic word for steam, is made in a distillery powered by geothermal energy, using water drawn from a 4000-year-old lava field.

It is also a country where everybody eats fish all the time. This recipe is inspired by Iceland.

CRÊPES

Mix the oil, egg and milk together, whisking until smooth. Sift the flour with the salt into a bowl and make a well in the centre. Add the liquid slowly, stirring all the time, until smooth. Leave it to stand for half an hour while you make the filling.

Heat a small non-stick pan over medium heat. Lightly oil the pan. Use a quarter cup measure to scoop out some crêpe mixture. Quickly swirl the pan as you pour it in, so it covers the bottom in a thin layer. Cook for a minute or 2, until the bottom is light brown. Flip over using a spatula and cook the other side. Keep warm while you cook all the crêpes. This makes 10 to 12 crêpes, depending on how thin you make them.

FILLING

Melt the butter in a large saucepan. Add the flour and stir until well mixed. Cook for 2 to 3 minutes and remove from heat. Add the milk slowly, stirring all the time so the flour is not lumpy. Add the paprika and salt and return to the heat, stirring as it thickens.

Add the cream cheese and stir until smooth. Add the vodka, salmon, broccoli, chives and nasturtium seeds. (For extra kick, use some horseradish vodka, see page 141.) Stir through and cook for a couple of minutes, then add black pepper to taste. Keep the filling warm while you cook the crêpes.

To serve, place a crêpe on a plate and add a dollop of salmon filling. Roll up and
garnish with a nasturtium flower.

V Vegetarian option: replace the salmon with sliced mushrooms.

CABBAGE

Although they are here under winter seasonal vegetables, cabbages can grow almost all year round. From monster varieties with loose, variegated leaves, to tiny, compact red ones, I always have a cabbage or three ripening in my garden.

They are equally versatile in the kitchen. The raw crunch of coleslaw makes the most of fresh cabbage's mustardy flavour, while cooked cabbage is mellow and sweet. Cabbage has the reputation of being smelly when cooked. But don't lay the blame on the cabbage – it is the cook who is more often at fault. Overcooked cabbage will result in a stinky kitchen. And if you overcook cabbage in an aluminium pan it is even worse. The solution? Cook until just tender and use stainless steel or cast iron pans.

Harvesting, buying and storing cabbage

A cabbage should be harvested when the head has reached full size and is firm and compact. Don't leave them too long otherwise they might split.

When buying cabbages, look for ones with their leaves still tight against the stem – if they are beginning to separate it is a sign of age. Cabbages can keep for a surprisingly long time in the fridge. Store them unwashed in a sealed plastic bag, and they will last for up to two weeks.

- 16 large cabbage leaves
- peanut oil
- 4 cloves garlic, diced
- 2 small red chillies, diced
- 500 g beef mince
- 2 tablespoons fish sauce
- 1 tablespoon dark soy sauce
- 1 tablespoon sugar
- 3 tablespoons water
- 10 sugar snap peas, cut in half
- ½ cup chopped mint
- olive oil
- extra chopped mint for sprinkling

SERVES 4

'Angel over Berlin' cabbage rolls

When we were in Berlin, we came across the exact street vendor who was featured in the Wim Wenders film *Angel over Berlin*. His speciality was German sausage, which he served with tender and tasty cabbage rolls. Most often made with pickled cabbage, they are a staple dish of many peasant cuisines in Europe and West Asia.

Peas and cabbages are at their sweetest in winter. Here they are combined with a spicy mince for a warming but fresh winter dish.

Prepare the cabbage by removing the thick base and steaming the leaves until just soft and pliable. While they are steaming, prepare the mince.

Heat the peanut oil in a wok over high heat until shimmering. Add the garlic and stir-fry for 15 to 20 seconds. Add the chillies and stir-fry for further 15 to 20 seconds. Then add the mince, stir-frying until it changes colour, and add the fish sauce, soy sauce, sugar and water. Stir to mix and simmer for 5 minutes. Add the peas and cook for a further minute or two. Stir in the mint and remove from the heat.

Heat the oven to 200°C. Place one cabbage leaf on a board and dollop a large spoon of mince at the stem end. Roll the leaf up, turning the sides in as you go so the mince is enclosed.

Place the rolls on a baking tray and drizzle with a little olive oil. Bake for 5 to 8 minutes. Sprinkle with extra chopped mint and serve with Tickled pink pickled red cabbage (see recipe on page 229).

V Vegetarian option: replace the mince with one cup of cooked rice mixed with two cups of cooked lentils. Replace the fish sauce with extra soy sauce.

CHICKEN

- 4 chicken breast fillets, skin removed
- 4 tablespoons Thai sweet chilli sauce (see page 94)
- 2 tablespoons ketjap manis (see page 250)
- 1 tablespoon sesame oil
- 8 slices of prosciutto
- 4 bamboo skewers, soaked in water for 30 minutes

SOM TAM CABBAGE SALAD

- 2 egg noodle nests
- 2 hot fresh red chillies
- 1 clove garlic, finely diced
- ¼ cup unsalted roast peanuts
- 1 cup carrots, thinly sliced
- 1½ tablespoons grated palm sugar
- 1½ tablespoons fish sauce
- 1½ tablespoons lime juice
- 2 cups finely sliced red and green cabbage

SERVES 4

Prosciutto wrapped sweet chilli chicken breasts with Som Tam cabbage salad

The first time I tasted Thai sweet chilli sauce was on Koh Tao island, Thailand, in 1991. We had spent the day snorkelling on coral reefs and were ravenous. Our boatman bought us skewers of chicken from a woman who was cooking them on the beach. They were served with a little bag of sweet chilli sauce. Sitting on white coral sand, watching the sky change colour as the sun set, we ate our skewers. The heavenly explosion of sweet, salty and hot is a taste that transports me back to that blissful moment.

Som Tam is a very popular Thai salad made with unripe papaya. In my version, I use cabbage as a crunchy, fresh alternative.

CHICKEN

Place the chicken breasts between sheets of cling wrap and bash them with a meat tenderiser. Don't make them too thin – you are aiming to just even them out. Mix the chilli sauce, ketjap manis and sesame oil in a shallow dish. Add the chicken breasts to the marinade and toss to coat.

Place 2 slices of prosciutto on a board and put a chicken breast on top. Wrap the prosciutto around the breast, securing it with the skewers. Wrap the remaining chicken fillets in the same way. Place them on a baking tray and grill for 8 to 10 minutes, turning and basting with the marinade occasionally, until the breasts are cooked and the prosciutto crisp. While the chicken is cooking, prepare the cabbage.

SOM TAM CABBAGE SALAD

Cook the noodles in salted, boiling water and as soon as they are cooked, rinse them with cold water and drain. Toss with a little oil and set aside.

Using a large pestle and mortar, grind the chillies and garlic together to form a chunky paste. Add the peanuts and pound until they are broken into chunks. Add the carrots, palm sugar, fish sauce and lime juice and mix them in well. Add the cabbage and pound lightly so the cabbage is just bruised and absorbs the flavour of the sauce. Serve over the cold egg noodles.

V Vegetarian option: replace the chicken with portions of haloumi cheese, toss with the marinade and wrap in vine leaves instead of prosciutto. Bake at 200°C for 10 to 15 minutes. Replace the fish sauce in the cabbage salad with soy sauce.

CAULIFLOWER

Cauliflower is great to grow and is pretty much hassle-free. There are several varieties to choose from – I once grew a cheddar cauliflower, although the name refers to its glorious orange colour, not to its taste.

The flavour of a freshly picked cauliflower is so vastly superior to a week-old supermarket one that it is certainly worth growing them. Even if you harvest only a few from a small garden, they are a treat.

Cauliflower is another vegetable with a wide variety of uses – from little raw florets dipped into spring onion-flavoured cream cheese, to smooth and creamy soups, it can do it all.

Harvesting, buying and storing cauliflower

Pick cauliflower once the 'curd' is fully exposed and none of the inner leaves are covering it. Cut it off at the stem, keeping several layers of leaves for protection. When shopping, look for cauliflower with tight florets and no discoloration. If there are leaves, they should be crisp and whole, not limp and battered.

Store them in a plastic bag in the fridge for about a week. Cauliflower freezes well. Cut it into florets first and then follow the procedure described on page 235.

CAULIFLOWER PURÉE

- 1 cup whole milk
- ¼ cup cream
- 3 cups cauliflower florets
- 1 small onion, finely chopped
- 100g creamy blue cheese
- 1 teaspoon chilli jelly (recipe on page 92)
- salt and pepper to taste
- 2 tablespoons green peppercorns, rinsed and drained

SERVES 4

Steak with cauliflower, blue cheese and green peppercorn purée

A wise Chinese chef once told me that just a pinch of sugar adds a magic tweak to any dish. But in this recipe, I use homemade chilli jelly, which lends subtle sweetness as well as a little heat. This creamy purée brings out the best of cauliflower's sweet taste and goes perfectly with blue cheese.

CAULIFLOWER PURÉE

Mix the milk and cream together in a large saucepan. Add the cauliflower and onion, cover and simmer for 10 to 15 minutes. Prepare the steak while the cauliflower is simmering.

When the cauliflower is tender, leave it to cool a little and purée with an immersion blender. Return to the heat and add the blue cheese, stirring until it has melted. Add the chilly jelly, salt and pepper to taste. Add the peppercorns and heat through.

STEAK

Pat steaks dry and slash any thicker, fat sections at even intervals. This will prevent the steaks from curling up while cooking. Sprinkle with the rub, patting it into the surface evenly. Leave covered for 10 to 15 minutes.

Place a cast iron pan on high heat. Heat the oil and add the steaks, fat side down first. (Lean them against the sides of the pan.) Cook the fat edges for about 2 to 3 minutes and then turn flat. Cook each side for 3 to 4 minutes for rare, and 5 to 6 for medium rare. Remove from heat, cover and leave to rest for 10 minutes.

V Vegetarian option: cut a cauliflower vertically into thick 4 cm slices, keeping the florets attached to the stem. Brush both sides with olive oil and sprinkle with a little steak rub, taking care not to break them. Spread onto a baking tray and grill for 8 to 10 minutes, turning half way through. Serve with the purée.

STEAK

- 800 g thick rump steak
- ½ cup steak rub (recipe on page 231)
- olive oil

Cauliflower cheese with a twist

Most often when I'm cooking cauliflower, I tend to think about all sorts of dishes and then land up cooking some version of cauliflower cheese. Here is a recipe that (surprise!) uses both — but not how you'd expect.

Heat the olive oil in a pan. Add the garlic and sauté until just softened. Add the cauliflower and pine nuts and stir gently until the cauliflower starts to brown. Add the chives, lemon juice and Parmesan cheese. Stir through until it is all mixed together and remove from heat. Add salt to taste.

- olive oil
- 3 garlic cloves, diced
- 1 head of cauliflower, cut into small florets
- 2 tablespoons pine nuts
- 2 tablespoons chopped chives
- lemon juice to taste
- ¼ cup Parmesan cheese, finely grated
- flaky sea salt to taste

SERVES 2 AS A SIDE DISH

PEAS

Peas, peas, glorious peas … my earliest memories of vegetable gardening are of picking and shelling green peas on my grandfather's farm when I was about three or four. They tasted better than any chocolate or sweet – and I had quite a sweet tooth.

Some varieties of peas can be eaten pod and all; others have to be shelled first. My favourites are sugar snap peas, where both the pea and pod are edible. Peas need to be cooked for only a very short time, otherwise they lose that glorious verdant colour and go a mushy grey-green.

Harvesting, buying and storing peas

Peas start maturing from the bottom of the plant first. Frequent harvesting encourages more pods to form. Peas should be eaten as soon as possible after harvesting otherwise they begin to lose their sweetness.

When choosing peas to buy, look for ones with bright green and shiny pods. If they are dull they have been sitting around for a while. Open pods are a no-no, it means they are overripe and won't taste at all sweet. Only shell the peas when you are ready to use them. Freezing peas is the best way to preserve their fresh flavour – a good way to enjoy this delicious vegetable all through the year. (See page 235 for details on freezing.)

- 1 litre ham stock
  (see page 233)
- 500 g freshly shelled peas
- salt and pepper to taste
- 1 cup of ham, chopped
  into chunks
- chopped fresh chives

SERVES 4

Green pea soup and ham

One year I was the one who received the ham bone from Christmas lunch and so I popped it into the freezer. A few months later, when the weather was cooler, out it came and I made about 4 litres of ham stock, which I froze. The delicious base of ham stock makes this deceptively simple soup taste far more complex than it is.

Heat the stock until it boils. Add the peas and bring back to the boil for about 2 to 3 minutes. Remove from the heat and, using an immersion blender, blend the soup until it is smooth and green. Return to the heat and bring back to a simmer. Add salt and pepper to taste.

Portion the ham and chives evenly in individual serving bowls. Pour soup over and serve with slices of crusty bread. (Tip: try to buy a whole piece of ham so that you can cut it into thick chunks rather than using deli-sliced ham.)

V Vegetarian option: slice 2 onions finely and cook in olive oil until just starting to brown. Add 1 litre of vegetable stock (see page 233) and continue with the recipe as above, leaving out the chunks of ham. Sprinkle with fried onion (see page 29) just before serving.

Turkish pea and yoghurt soup drizzled with mint and pine nut oil

My Turkish step-mother-in-law, Sevim, cooks delicious traditional Turkish food. When we stayed with her for a few weeks in Memphis, I learned quite a few tricks in her kitchen.

I would never have thought of cooking yoghurt – but it works and is a delicious comfort soup. Pine nuts are not the cheapest ingredient but they have such a distinctive taste and you don't have to use all that many to flavour this dish.

SOUP

- ¼ cup long-grain rice
- 1 litre stock
- 1 cup freshly shelled peas
- ¼ cup mint leaves
- 1 tablespoon butter
- 2 tablespoons flour
- 1 egg
- 2 cups plain yoghurt
- 2 tablespoons water
- pinch of sugar
- salt and pepper to taste

MINT AND PINE NUT OIL

- ¼ cup pine nuts
- 2 tablespoons butter
- ¼ cup finely chopped mint

SERVES 4

SOUP

Rinse the rice well until the water runs clear. Mix the stock and rice together in a large pot and bring to the boil. (You can use beef, chicken or vegetable stock for this soup.) Reduce the heat and simmer until the rice is very soft, 25 to 30 minutes.

While the rice is cooking, bring another pot of salted water to the boil. Add the peas and mint and bring back to the boil. Cook for a few minutes and then drain. Blend until smooth. Add the butter and blend again. Keep the pea and mint purée warm while you finish off the soup.

Beat the flour and egg together well in a bowl. Add the yoghurt and water, and mix until smooth. Scoop a couple of spoons of broth from the rice pot and add it to the yoghurt mixture, stirring it in well. Add the yoghurt mixture very slowly to the broth, stirring as you pour. Bring it back to a simmer and cook for 10 more minutes. (Make the mint and pine nut oil while it is cooking.) Add a pinch of sugar, and salt and pepper to taste.

Swirl the pea and mint purée through the soup, so it creates green streaks. Drizzle with some of the mint and pine nut oil, and serve with crusty olive bread on the side.

MINT AND PINE NUT OIL

Dry-fry the pine nuts in a cast iron frying pan until just starting to brown. Add the butter and as soon as it starts sizzling add the mint. Stir quickly and pour into a dipping bowl.

WINTER SQUASH

Versatile winter squash are a must-have in my kitchen. There are orange, green, yellow and white ones, and they can be quickly steamed or slow-cooked, puréed, blended or sliced. They are perfectly suited to the dishes I crave in colder weather – hearty roast vegetables, warming soups and spicy curries.

Harvesting, buying and storing winter squash

Even though they are grown during the warm summer months, squash, butternut, pumpkin and others, are called winter squash because they can be stored for many months after being harvested. Coming in a variety of shapes and sizes, they have in common a thick skin. The harder the skin, the longer they will keep.

Leave squash until the vine has withered and the skin has thickened and hardened – if you can't scratch it with your fingernail, it is ready. Unlike summer squash, the flavour gets better the longer they ripen. Cut the squash off the vine leaving 5 to 10 cm of stem. Be gentle when handling them – bruised or broken patches will spoil quickly. Store them in a dry spot with good air circulation.

Lucky butternut soup

Penang Island in Malaysia is a food lover's haven. Street-side hawkers offer an endless variety of Malay, Chinese and Indian cuisine. Vegetarian curries served on banana leaf platters, crispy tandoori chicken with naan bread, creamy laksa soup and noodles, and citrus pancakes with coconut topping are just a few of the many dishes on offer.

The Chinese New Year was celebrated while we were there. Because the Chinese word for 'orange' sounds very similar to 'luck', it is considered good luck to give oranges to friends and to eat orange food during the celebrations. This soup was one of the many orange meals we ate that week – bringing us plenty of luck! The glorious colour of this soup is sunshine in a bowl, just what we need in winter.

Preheat the oven to 200°C. Toss the onion, ginger, garlic, butternut and carrots with the olive oil, spices and salt to taste. Spread out on a baking tray and roast for 30 to 45 minutes, turning occasionally.

Bring the chicken stock to the boil over medium heat. Remove the roast vegetables from the oven and add to the stock. Add the wine to the roasting pan and place it over a low heat. Stir, scraping up any stuck and caramelised bits. Add to the pot. Add the orange juice, bring to the boil and simmer for 5 to 7 minutes.

Remove from the stove and purée with an immersion blender until the soup is smooth. Return to the heat, add salt and pepper to taste, and bring back to a simmer.

Divide amongst individual bowls with a drizzle of yoghurt, sprinkled with orange zest, coriander and spring onions.

- 1 large onion, sliced
- 3 cm ginger, peeled and cut into thick slices
- 3 cloves garlic, halved
- 1 large butternut, peeled, seeded and cut into small chunks
- 2 carrots, roughly chopped
- olive oil
- 1 tablespoon coriander
- 2 teaspoons cumin
- salt to taste
- 1 litre chicken stock
- 2 tablespoons white wine
- ¼ cup fresh orange juice
- salt and pepper to taste
- ¼ cup plain yoghurt
- 3 tablespoons orange zest
- ½ cup coriander leaves
- 5 spring onions, thinly sliced

SERVES 4

- 1 cup dried red kidney beans
- olive oil
- 1 onion, sliced
- 1 cup butternut or pumpkin, cut into small chunks
- 2 large garlic cloves, diced
- 2 small dried chillies, finely chopped
- 500 g lean minced beef
- 1 tablespoon fresh oregano
- 2 teaspoons cumin
- ½ teaspoon black pepper, freshly ground
- 1 teaspoon paprika
- ½ teaspoon hot chilli powder
- kernels from 1 sweet corn cob
- 3 x 410 ml bottles Mexican tomatoes (page 226)
- a teaspoon or so of salt
- pinch of sugar
- squeeze of lime
- 8 flour tortillas
- 1 cup grated cheddar
- 1 cup grated mozzarella

SERVES 8

Mexican beef, bean and squash enchiladas

I love the combination and play of flavours in Mexican food – hearty beans with sprightly tomatoes, spiced meat with sweet squash and mellow avocado.

This enchilada recipe is simple to make. It is also an easy make-ahead meal for a large party. They can be prepared up to the point of being cooked. Cover the baking tray tightly with aluminium foil and chill. Cook them while guests are eating starters or having snacks and drinks.

Cook the beans according to the instructions on page 249 and set aside. If you prefer to use tinned beans, use a can of red kidney beans, rinsed and drained.

Preheat the oven to 200°C. Heat the oil in a heavy-bottomed pot. Add the onion and cook, stirring occasionally, for about 5 minutes over medium heat, until soft. Add the squash and cook until just browned. Add the garlic and chilli and cook for a further minute or so. Add the beef and cook, stirring to break it up, until it changes colour from pink to brown. Season with oregano, cumin, pepper, paprika and chilli powder. Continue cooking for 3 minutes.

Add the sweet corn kernels, two of the bottles of Mexican tomatoes and the cooked beans. Bring to the boil and simmer for 5 minutes. Season with salt to taste, and stir in the sugar and lime juice.

Place a large spoonful of the mixture at the bottom of a flour tortilla. Roll it up, folding the sides in to enclose the filling. Place in a large roasting pan. Repeat until all the tortillas are full. Spoon the remaining bottle of Mexican tomato evenly over the top and cover with cheddar and mozzarella cheese.

Place in the oven and bake for 10 to 12 minutes until bubbling and the cheese has browned. Serve immediately.

Pass around the accompaniments separately so that guests can help themselves.

V Vegetarian option: instead of the beef mince, add 1 cup of black beans (cooked according to the instructions on page 249). Increase the sweet corn to 3 cobs and the cups of squash to 2.

ACCOMPANIMENTS

- 1 bowl cos lettuce leaves, sliced into ribbons
- 1 large avocado pear, cut into bite-sized pieces
- 500 ml sour cream
- pickled jalapenos, sliced
- fresh coriander

THE WINTER PANTRY

My friends tease me about my bomb shelter pantry. I have shelves piled high with dried beans, bottled tomatoes, jams, jellies, preserves, anchovies, olives, rice, pasta and much, much more. It's not that I believe the end of the world is nigh — it's because there is always another dinner just around the corner. Having a well-stocked pantry means you are never limited for choice and are prepared for unexpected dinner guests.

Winter is the perfect time to make use of pantry supplies in hearty slow-cooked meals that warm up the kitchen and fill the house with rich, spicy aromas. It is also the season to enjoy spending time indoors, making fudge, preserves and flavoursome soup stocks.

Harvesting, buying and storing for the winter pantry

Harvest ingredients for bottling when they are ripe and ready. At your local greengrocer or farmers market, seasonal vegetables are usually much cheaper. Buy them in bulk and bottle or dry them for your pantry. Have a look at the Harvest Recipes starting on page 224 for some ideas. Make sure you use airtight containers and place a bay leaf in any dried goods to help deter bugs.

Yosemite baked beans and pork

We visited Yosemite National Park in mid-October. This park straddles the Sierra Nevada and was the most interesting route from San Francisco to Tucson, Arizona. We were camping but weren't prepared for the icy temperatures at nearly 2 000 metres above sea level. We gave up any idea of cooking outdoors and braved the food court's 'eat as much as you like' buffet. Some of the food was awful but the hearty slow-cooked pork and beans was a perfect dish for a chilly winter's night.

After making this, you'll never want to open a can of bought baked beans again. To make a lighter version as a side dish for a summer braai, leave out the pork fillet.

- 2 cups dried cannellini beans
- olive oil
- 10 rashers streaky bacon
- 1 onion, diced
- 4 garlic cloves, diced
- 800 g pork fillet
- 1 Granny Smith apple, cored, peeled and diced
- 250 ml chicken stock
- 1½ tablespoons hot English mustard powder
- ¼ teaspoon grated nutmeg
- ⅛ teaspoon ground cloves
- black pepper
- 2 teaspoons Tabasco
- 2 tablespoons maple syrup
- 1 cup tomato sauce
- 3 teaspoons dried marjoram
- 2 teaspoons apple cider vinegar
- 1 tablespoon Worcestershire sauce

SERVES 8

It you use dried cannellini beans prepare them according to the instructions on page 249, and set aside. If you prefer to use tinned beans, you will need 2 cans of cannellini beans, rinsed and drained.

Heat the oven to 180°C. Heat olive oil in a cast iron pot and cook the bacon for about 5 minutes. Remove from the pot and set aside, leaving the bacon fat in the pot. Add the onions and cook until soft. Add the garlic and cook for a minute. Cut the pork into 2 cm cubes, and cook until it changes colour. Then add the cooked beans and diced apple, and stir through.

Keeping the bacon aside, mix the remaining ingredients together until smooth and pour into the pot. Stir so that everything is well coated and bring to the boil. Pour into a large, shallow baking dish. Cover the top with the bacon rashers and bake for about 45 minutes.

V Vegetarian option: replace the pork with an additional cup of beans. Instead of bacon, cut two potatoes into thick slices, parboil them and drain. Brush them with olive oil and sprinkle with salt before layering on top of the beans.

- 2 tablespoons olive oil
- I onion, diced
- 500 g beef mince
- I tablespoon fresh thyme, chopped
- I tablespoon fresh rosemary, chopped
- I tablespoon dried oregano
- I teaspoon salt
- I tablespoon fresh basil, chopped
- ¼ teaspoon freshly ground black pepper
- I teaspoon Worcestershire sauce
- ½ teaspoon brown sugar
- I tablespoon butter
- 800 ml bottled tomatoes (see page 225)
- I small can tomato paste
- salt to taste
- spaghetti
- grated Parmesan cheese

SERVES 4

Speedy spaghetti bolognaise

When I came home from university for the holidays, the first meal Mom would make for me would be spaghetti bolognaise. Slow cooked for hours, the bolognaise was rich and meaty with a robust tomato sauce. It still remains my favourite dish of Mom's. Here is my quick everyday version.

Heat the olive oil in a large, heavy-bottomed pot. Add the onion and cook, stirring occasionally, for 6 to 8 minutes until browned and soft. Add the mince and cook, stirring until it changes colour. Add the herbs, seasoning, Worcestershire sauce, sugar and butter. Cook for a further 2 to 3 minutes.

Push the tomatoes through a sieve, using a wooden spoon to break up the pieces. Add to the pot and stir through. Add the tomato paste. Bring to the boil then turn down the heat and simmer uncovered while the pasta is cooking. Add salt to taste.

Bring a large pot of salted water to the boil. Add a splash of olive oil and sufficient spaghetti for 4 people. Bring back to the boil and cook for 12 to 15 minutes until *al dente*. Remove from the heat, drain and serve topped with bolognaise sauce and grated Parmesan cheese.

V Vegetarian option: replace the mince with 1 large eggplant and 2 carrots, finely ground in a food processor.

Pink delight guavas

When I was a child, Mom was always busy preserving and bottling the fruit that grew in her garden. (And in her eighties she still does!) The kumquat tree was especially abundant and I remember one year she experimented with preserving kumquats in brandy. The hard little orangey-brown balls were inedible, but the kumquat-drenched brandy, drizzled over her homemade ice cream, was superb.

Mom has taught me never to be afraid to experiment – and to make the most of surprise results. This recipe is for my mother.

Add the rosé and berry juice to a pot (use 100% pure, unsweetened juice). Split the vanilla pods open and scrape the seeds into the pot. Then add the pods, sugars and verjuice. Bring to the boil, stirring to dissolve the sugar.

Add the guavas and maintain a gentle simmer. Cover and poach for 10 minutes. Either serve immediately with some cream or ice cream, or pour into sterilised bottles and seal (see page 239).

If you have an abundance of other fruit – such as pears, peaches, nectarines, plums, apples or apricots – they would all work well for this recipe.

- 2 cups dry rosé wine
- ½ cup mixed berry juice
- 2 vanilla pods
- ½ cup vanilla sugar (see page 101)
- ½ cup lemon verbena sugar (see page 101)
- ¼ cup verjuice
- 6 guavas, peeled and halved

SERVES 6

HARVEST RECIPES

It was only when I was faced with the abundance of my first harvest, that I realised how rewarding it is to make the most of what our gardens provide. Pickles and preserves, jams and chutneys, spice rubs and curry pastes – all ensure that seasonal flavours are savoured in the kitchen throughout the year.

BOTTLED TOMATOES

Bottled tomatoes are endlessly useful, and there is something deeply satisfying about opening a bottle of home-grown summer tomatoes in the heart of winter.

Basic bottled tomatoes

- 4 kg tomatoes
- 1 tablespoon sea salt
- 4 tablespoons lemon juice
- pinch sugar

Wash and dry the tomatoes. (If you want peeled tomatoes follow the method on page 236). Slice in half, put them in a large pot and add the salt. Bring to the boil and simmer uncovered for 5 minutes, stirring occasionally. Add the lemon juice and stir through.

If you want puréed tomatoes, process them with a stick blender before bottling.

Fill sterilised bottles (see page 239) and seal well. The lemon juice ensures that it is acidic enough to deter spoilage.

When adding them to a dish, add a pinch of sugar to counteract the acidity.

Indian flavoured tomatoes

- 4 kg tomatoes
- 3 onions, finely chopped
- 4 cloves garlic, chopped
- 2 small chillies, chopped
- 1 tablespoon ground coriander
- 1 tablespoon ground cumin
- 2 teaspoons turmeric
- 2 tablespoons curry leaves
- 1 tablespoon sea salt
- 4 tablespoons lemon juice

Wash and dry the tomatoes, then chop them roughly. Put them in a large pot together with the rest of the ingredients, except for the lemon juice. Bring to the boil and simmer uncovered for 10 minutes, stirring occasionally until thickened. Add the lemon juice and stir through. Fill sterilised bottles (see page 239).

Italian flavoured tomatoes

- 4 kg tomatoes
- 4 onions, finely chopped
- 2 cloves garlic, chopped
- 2 tablespoons oregano, chopped
- 3 tablespoons fresh flat leaf parsley, chopped
- 1 tablespoon sea salt
- 2 tablespoons sugar
- ½ cup fresh basil, chopped
- 4 tablespoons lemon juice

Wash and dry the tomatoes, then chop them roughly. Put them in a large pot together with the rest of the ingredients, except for the fresh basil and lemon juice.

Bring to the boil and simmer uncovered for 10 minutes, stirring occasionally, until thickened. Add the fresh basil and lemon juice and stir through until mixed.

Fill sterilised bottles (see page 239) and seal well.

Mexican flavoured tomatoes

- 4 kg tomatoes
- 2 onions, finely chopped
- 6 cloves garlic, chopped
- 2 jalapeno chillies, chopped
- 1 tablespoon fresh oregano
- 1 teaspoon ground cumin
- 1 tablespoon sea salt
- 1 teaspoon sugar
- ½ cup fresh coriander, chopped
- 4 tablespoons lemon juice

Wash and dry the tomatoes, then chop them roughly. Add the rest of the ingredients to the tomatoes, except for the fresh coriander and lemon juice. Bring to the boil and simmer uncovered for 10 minutes, stirring occasionally, until thickened. Add the fresh coriander and lemon juice and stir through until mixed. Fill sterilised bottles (see page 239) with the tomatoes and seal well.

CHUTNEY

I first started making chutney when I had an excess of both plums and chillies. They worked so well that I started making chutney with other ingredients. South Africa's most famous chutney is Mrs Balls. I decided she was having far too much fun, so I named my chutney range Mrs Boobs.

Butternut, orange and ginger chutney

This sweet and spicy chutney is a gorgeous orange and is delicious with curries.

- 2 oranges
- 1 tablespoon lime pips
- 2 kg butternut, peeled and diced
- 3 tablespoons grated ginger
- 1½ cups water
- ⅓ cup lime juice
- 1½ kg sugar
- 5 red chillies, deseeded and finely chopped

Cut the oranges into quarters and remove the pips. Tie the orange pips with the lime pips in a muslin bag or put them inside a tea strainer that closes. The pips contain plenty of pectin – the stuff that will make the chutney set.

Slice the oranges finely. Place the oranges and the pips in a large pot with the butternut, ginger, water and lime juice and bring to the boil. Reduce heat and simmer covered, until the butternut is soft.

Add the sugar and chillies and stir over a low heat until the sugar has dissolved. Bring back to the boil and cook until it is set. Pour into sterilised bottles (see page 239) and seal.

Sweet potato and habanero chutney

This habanero chutney is hot – but the heat is balanced by the sweet potato. Try substituting the sweet potato with plums and the habanero with a milder chilli.

- 1 kg sweet potatoes
- 500 g apples
- 5 cm piece fresh ginger
- 2 onions, sliced
- 1 cup apple cider vinegar
- ¼ cup lime juice
- ½ cup raisins
- 1 habanero chilli, chopped
- 1 tablespoon mustard seeds
- 3 garlic cloves, chopped
- 2 teaspoons cinnamon
- 2 teaspoons coriander seeds, dry toasted
- 2 teaspoons cumin seeds, dry toasted
- 1 teaspoon mustard powder
- 1 teaspoon soy sauce
- 1 teaspoon Worcestershire sauce
- 1 teaspoon salt
- 2 cups brown sugar

Peel the sweet potatoes and apples, and chop into small chunks. Peel the ginger and chop finely. Put everything except the sugar into a large pot and cook until soft. Add the sugar and stir until dissolved.

Bring to the boil, reduce heat and simmer for an hour, stirring often until thickened. Ladle into hot sterilised bottles (see page 239) and seal. Refrigerate once it is opened. Delicious served with Quick chicken curry (see page 150).

PASTES

The following pastes are easy to make and taste so much better than bought ones. Because a good paste takes a bit of time to prepare, it is worth making a big batch and storing it in the freezer. Don't forget to label and date the containers.

Green curry paste

- 1 tablespoon coriander seeds, toasted
- 1 teaspoon cumin seeds, toasted
- 5 peppercorns
- 4 stalks lemon grass, peeled and sliced
- 4 cm piece ginger, peeled and roughly chopped
- 5 cloves garlic, roughly chopped
- 5 spring onions
- ¼ cup coriander root, stems and leaves
- 1 teaspoon lime zest
- ½ cup fresh hot green chillies
- 1 teaspoon salt
- 1 teaspoon shrimp paste
- peanut oil

Combine the coriander seeds, cumin and peppercorns in a spice grinder and crush to a powder. Place all the ingredients in a food processor and grind until well blended, adding a little peanut oil if needed. Scoop into an airtight container and freeze.

Red curry paste

- ½ cup dried red chillies
- 1 tablespoon coriander seeds, toasted
- 1 teaspoon cumin seeds, toasted
- 10 peppercorns
- 4 stalks lemon grass
- 4 cm piece ginger, peeled and roughly chopped
- 4 cloves garlic, roughly chopped
- 8 spring onions
- 1 tablespoon coriander root
- 1 teaspoon lime zest
- 1 teaspoon salt
- 1 teaspoon shrimp paste

Remove the stems from the chillies and shake out most of the seeds. Chop them up roughly and then soak them in warm water for 20 minutes. Combine the coriander seeds, cumin and peppercorns in a spice grinder and crush to a powder.

Remove the chillies from the water and reserve the soaking liquid. Peel and slice the lemongrass. Place the chillies, the ground seeds and all remaining ingredients in a food processor. Grind until a paste forms, adding some of the soaking liquid if needed. Scoop into an airtight container and freeze.

Roast garlic paste

Roasted garlic is far mellower than raw or quickly cooked garlic. It can be added to pasta sauces and soups or eaten as a starter on crisp toast with onion marmalade on the side. It can also be made into a paste.

To roast garlic, use whole bulbs. Cut the top off, exposing the cloves. Wrap aluminium foil around them, drizzling with olive oil before twisting the top shut. Bake at 180° C for 45 minutes to 1 hour. The cloves will be soft and tender, and easy to squeeze out of their skins. Either use immediately or mash them together with the oil from the baking tray, adding salt to taste and extra olive oil, to form a paste. Store in the fridge for up to a week.

PRESERVES AND PICKLES

Once you have learnt the basics of how to preserve and pickle, you can experiment with different ingredients. For a creative cook there are endless variations to try.

Cauliflower piccalilli
- 1 cucumber, deseeded and chopped
- 1 cauliflower, cut into florets
- 2 carrots, peeled and sliced
- 1 tablespoon sea salt
- 1 tablespoon celery salt
- 350 ml white wine vinegar
- 175 ml malt vinegar
- 2 tablespoons hot English mustard powder
- 175 g caster sugar
- 2 teaspoons ground turmeric
- 4 teaspoons cornflour

Mix the vegetables in a colander together with the salts. (If the cucumber has a thick skin, peel it.) Set the colander over a bowl and leave for an hour. Rinse the vegetables and discard the liquid.

Boil the vinegars together and leave to cool slightly. Mix the mustard powder, caster sugar, turmeric and cornflour together in a large pan. Add the vinegar to this mixture, whisking it in slowly so it doesn't become lumpy. Cook over a low heat, stirring, until the sauce thickens slightly. Let it cook for about 2 to 3 minutes more. Add the vegetables to the sauce and mix well. Pack into sterilised jars (see page 239) and seal.

Pickled broccoli
- 1 tablespoon olive oil
- 1 teaspoon cumin seeds
- 1 tablespoon garlic, diced
- 2 chillies, sliced
- 5 cm fresh ginger, peeled and finely chopped
- ⅛ teaspoon turmeric
- ⅔ cup white wine vinegar
- 2½ cups water
- 200 g broccoli, cut into florets
- 1 large red pepper, deseeded and sliced
- 2 teaspoons sea salt

In a large pan, heat the oil over low heat and add the cumin seeds. As soon as they start releasing their fragrance, add the garlic, chillies, ginger and turmeric.

Cook, stirring occasionally, for about 3 minutes. Add the vinegar and water to the pan, turn up the heat and bring to the boil.

Add the broccoli, red pepper and salt and boil for 2 to 3 minutes. Remove from the heat and pack the vegetables into sterilised bottles, adding enough vinegar cooking liquid to completely cover them.

Shake the bottles gently to remove any air bubbles, and seal.

Preserved ginger in lemon grass syrup

My grandfather was born on Christmas Day. He lived to just shy of 105 years. As the youngest granddaughter it was my job to help him open his pile of presents. One of his favourite gifts was preserved ginger – along with homemade fudge. This recipe is in memory of Pa.

- 1½ cups water
- 1½ cups sugar
- 300 g young ginger, peeled
- 2 stalks lemon grass
- 2 tablespoons verjuice syrup

Mix the water and sugar in a small heavy-bottomed pot over medium heat, stirring occasionally until dissolved. Cut the ginger into thin slices and add to the sugar syrup. Cut the lemon grass stalks into 3 cm lengths and bruise. Add to the pot. Boil gently for about 50 minutes, stirring occasionally, until the liquid has reduced by about half and the ginger is almost transparent. Add the verjuice syrup and boil gently for a further 15 minutes. Pour into sterilised bottles (see page 239) and seal. Try this as a topping on ice cream or accompanying ripe Brie or Camembert. (Makes about 2 cups.)

Tickled pink pickled red cabbage

Red cabbage should really be called purple and this pickled dish makes the most of its glorious colour. Crisp, sweet and sour, this pickle is delicious with cold meat or cheese.

- 2 baby red cabbages
- 2 carrots, peeled
- 1 tablespoon dill seeds
- 2 cups water
- ¼ cup honey
- ¾ cup white wine vinegar
- 1 tablespoon salt
- ¼ cup olive oil

Slice the cabbage and carrots finely and mix well together. Whisk the dill, water, honey, vinegar, salt and oil together. Fill a sterilised bottle (see page 239) with the cabbage and carrot mix. Add the vinegar mixture until it covers the vegetables. Seal and, before serving, keep in the fridge for a couple of days for the flavours to blend. Delicious served with 'Angel over Berlin' cabbage rolls (see page 196).

SPICE MIXES

I like experimenting with spice mixes, blending dried chillies, herbs and spices together to create unique and interesting flavours. These blends work best with fresh whole spices, which are often roasted first (see page 238). It helps to have a blender or electric coffee grinder but you can use a spice bottle with a grinding lid. Store spice blends in an airtight container for 3 to 4 months. Spice mixes are a great way of making

an otherwise ordinary dish exciting. I add them to egg dishes, soups, sautéed vegetables, slow-roasted vegetables as well as using them as rubs on meat.

Cajun spice

Originating from Louisiana in the United States, Cajun cuisine is an intriguing blend of French, Canadian and African influences, characterised by the use of fresh local ingredients. This spice mix is particularly good rubbed onto meat, chicken or fish before braaing or grilling. It can be used as a substitute for ordinary pepper to add an interesting twist to any dish.

- 1 tablespoon coriander seeds
- 2 whole dried red chillies, stems and seeds removed
- 1 tablespoon whole black peppercorns
- ¼ teaspoon cumin seeds
- 2 tablespoons salt
- 2 tablespoons paprika
- 1 tablespoon dried garlic
- 1 tablespoon dried oregano
- 2 teaspoons dried thyme

Dry roast the first 4 ingredients over a slow heat until fragrant. Grind all the roast spices to a powder and mix together with the remaining ingredients.

Citrus and herb spice rub

This blend is delicious rubbed on fish or chicken. Use it quickly as it loses its pungency after a month or two. Mix it with melted butter and toss with steamed asparagus or add it to yoghurt and mayonnaise to make a tartare sauce with a difference.

- 2 tablespoons whole black peppercorns
- 2 teaspoons sesame seeds
- 1 tablespoon lime zest
- 1 tablespoon orange zest
- 2 tablespoons dried thyme leaves
- 2 tablespoons dried mint leaves
- ½ teaspoon cinnamon
- 2 teaspoons hot paprika
- 2 teaspoons sea salt

Mix the peppercorns, sesame seeds and zest together and roast the mixture over a very slow heat until it becomes fragrant and the zest darkens. Remove from heat and grind in a spice grinder. Mix together with the remaining ingredients. Store in an airtight container.

Dukkah

There are many different recipes for dukkah, but they all contain a mixture of nuts, seeds and spices.

Try using almonds instead of hazelnuts and adding a little chilli to give it a bite. Delicious sprinkled over salads, rubbed onto meat before cooking, or simply as a dip with crusty bread and olive oil.

- 1 cup hazelnuts
- 1 cup almonds
- ¼ cup white sesame seeds
- 1 tablespoon coriander seeds
- 1 tablespoon cumin seeds
- 1 teaspoon sea salt
- 1 teaspoon coarsely ground black pepper

Roast the hazelnuts and almonds, then whiz in a food processor until coarsely ground. Tip into a bowl.

Toast the sesame seeds in a cast iron frying pan until golden and add to the nuts. Toast the coriander and cumin seeds in the same frying pan until fragrant and then grind in a spice grinder. Add to the bowl. Mix the salt and pepper through until the mixture is evenly blended. Store in an airtight container.

Garam masala

Although *garam masala* literally means 'hot mix', hot chilli powder is seldom an ingredient in traditional blends.

Garam refers to the aromatic and warm spices the mixture contains.

Used extensively in Indian cooking, there are as many recipes for this spicy mix as there are Bollywood films. This mix is used as a base for many curry recipes. It is also delicious sprinkled onto vegetables or added to a potato salad mix.

- 2 tablespoons cumin seeds
- 2 tablespoons coriander seeds
- 1 teaspoon cardamom pods
- 2 tablespoons black peppercorns
- 5 cm stick cinnamon
- ½ teaspoon whole cloves
- 1 piece star anise
- 1 teaspoon grated nutmeg

Mix all the spices (except the nutmeg) together in a heavy frying pan and roast over slow heat until they start becoming fragrant and darker. Remove from heat and cool. Remove the seeds from the cardamom pods and discard the pods. Grind all the roast spices to a powder and mix together with the nutmeg. Store in an airtight container.

Jane's delicious curry blend

This fragrant and spicy curry blend is one of my favourites. Adjust the heat by adding more or less chilli to your taste. This versatile curry mix can be used to add an Indian flavour to meat and vegetables or use it to tart up an egg dish (such as Eggs in a Hole on page 52). It can also be mixed with mayonnaise and salt to taste to make a yummy curry dip.

- 2 tablespoons coriander seeds
- 1 tablespoon cumin seeds
- 2 teaspoons fennel seeds
- 1 tablespoon whole fenugreek
- 4 whole cloves
- 2 cm cinnamon bark
- 4 cardamom pods
- 1 piece star anise
- 1 teaspoon peppercorns
- 3 whole dried red chillies, stems and seeds removed
- 1 tablespoon turmeric powder

Dry roast all the ingredients (except the turmeric powder) over a slow heat until fragrant. Remove from heat and cool. Grind to a powder and mix with the turmeric powder. Store in an airtight container.

Steak rub

I am never without a bottle of this near my stove and it is my 'go to' spice whenever I am cooking meat. Don't smother the meat with the rub, just sprinkle it all over and pat it on until the surface is evenly covered. Leaving the meat to stand for half an hour or so before cooking will improve the flavour. This is delicious rubbed onto beef or ostrich steaks.

- 2 tablespoons Japanese chilli powder
- 2 tablespoons ground pure coffee
- 2 tablespoons brown sugar
- 1 tablespoon coriander seeds, ground
- 2 teaspoons dried oregano
- 1½ teaspoons sea salt
- 1½ teaspoons coarsely ground black pepper

Mix all the ingredients together and store in an airtight container.

SOUP STOCKS

Homemade stocks add incredible depth of flavour to soups and stews. They are not difficult to make and don't take a lot of time. I have found the most practical way is to make a large amount of stock at one time and freeze it in 500 ml and 1 litre zip lock bags. The stock lasts for months in the freezer and it means that I can make a delicious (and nutritious) soup in about 15 minutes flat.

Beef stock

Beef stock is slightly more complicated than chicken stock as it involves roasting the ingredients first. But it is worth the extra effort as roasting creates a stock with far more depth.

- meaty beef bones
- onions
- celery
- carrots
- olive oil
- bay leaves
- peppercorns
- herbs

Heat oven to 200° C. Place the bones (any meaty bones can be used) on a baking tray and roast for about an hour, turning occasionally. While the bones are roasting, prepare the vegetables.

Peel and roughly chop some onions. Roughly chop some celery and carrots. Heat a little olive oil in a large pot and add the onions and carrots, stirring occasionally until the onions just start to brown. Add the celery and cook for a further 2 to 3 minutes.

Add the roasted bones to the pot and cover with water. Add some bay leaves, peppercorns and herbs, such as rosemary, thyme and parsley. If you would like an Asian flavoured stock, add some ginger, spring onions, lemon grass and star anise instead.

Bring to the boil and reduce to a simmer. Place the roasting pan you used to roast the bones over a burner and add a little water. As the water begins to simmer, scrape off any cooked bits. Pour the pan liquid into the stock pot. Cover and cook over a very low heat for about 6 hours. (Use a slow cooker if you have one.) Once the stock has cooled, follow the same procedure as for freezing chicken stock (see next recipe).

Chicken stock

Instead of using a chicken carcass, I poach a whole chicken. I then have a supply of cooked chicken meat to use in a variety of dishes plus a rich stock. Here's how.

- **whole chicken**
- **carrots**
- **onions**
- **celery**
- **herbs**
- **spices**
- **peppercorns**

Rinse the chicken well and cut off any pieces of hanging fat. Put the chicken into a large pot. Add some vegetables to flavour the stock. The standard ones are carrots, onions and celery, but you can also add garlic, parsnips and turnips. It is better to peel the onions and garlic first. Roughly chop all the vegetables, filling the chicken's cavity with some and placing the rest in the pot.

Add some herbs and spices to the pot. Again this depends on your taste. The classic ones are bay leaves, parsley, marjoram and thyme. If you are making an Asian stock, try adding ginger, lemon grass and lime leaves.

Depending on the flavour you are aiming for you can also add some sliced fruit, such as lemons or oranges. Add peppercorns and any other spices you want.

Cover the chicken with water and bring it to the boil. Reduce to just a simmer and cover the pot. Simmer for about 2 hours, until the meat pulls off the bone easily. Leave to cool in the pot. Take the chicken out and remove all the meat and keep in the fridge or freeze. Reserve the carcass. Scoop the fat off the surface of the broth and use it for thickening sauces (see page 239).

Pour the broth, a bit at a time, through a strainer into a measuring jug. Pour measured amounts into zip lock bags and seal them airtight using a straw (see page 238). Label and date the contents. Line a baking tray with paper towels and place the bags flat on the tray, with paper towels between each layer to stop them from sticking to one another. Freeze, and once they are solid they can be removed from the baking tray and stored in a freezer drawer.

If you have the energy after making the first batch, you can use the carcass to make a second batch of stock, as there will be plenty of flavour in the bones. Use this method if you have cooked a whole roast chicken. Put the carcass along with vegetables, herbs and peppercorns in a pot and cover with water. Bring to the boil. Skim off any froth from the surface and reduce to a simmer.

Simmer covered, for 3 to 4 hours, skimming occasionally. Follow the same procedure described above for pouring into bags.

Ham Stock

Delicious ham stock is far more full-bodied than any other stock, with layers of flavours. A ten-minute soup made with ham stock will taste as if you have slaved for hours over it.

- meaty ham bone
- carrots
- leeks
- onions
- peppercorns
- bay leaves

Place the meaty ham bone in a large pot along with some roughly chopped carrots, leeks and onions (peeled). Add a sprinkling of peppercorns and a few bay leaves, cover with water and bring to the boil.

Skim the scum off the surface and reduce the heat to a simmer. Cook covered for about 3 hours, skimming the surface occasionally.

Once the stock has cooled, follow the same procedure as for freezing chicken stock (see previous recipe).

Vegetable stock

The roasted vegetables give this simple stock a wonderful flavour.

- 1 head garlic
- 4 carrots, cut into chunks
- 4 potatoes, cut into chunks
- 4 celery stalks, cut into chunks
- 4 peeled onions, cut into chunks
- olive oil
- 8 cups water
- 2 teaspoons fresh thyme
- 2 teaspoons fresh parsley
- 2 bay leaves

Heat the oven to 200°C. Slice the top off the head of garlic and drizzle with olive oil. Wrap it in aluminium foil and place it on a baking tray. Drizzle the remaining vegetables with olive oil and place on the same baking tray. Roast for about an hour, turning occasionally.

Combine the water, thyme, parsley and bay leaves in a large pot over medium-high heat. Squeeze the garlic into the pot and discard the outer husks. Add the roast vegetables to the pot and bring to a boil. Reduce heat to low and simmer for 2 hours. Remove from heat and strain. Once the stock has cooled, follow the same procedure as for freezing chicken stock (see page 232).

TECHNIQUES & TIPS

A PRACTICAL KITCHEN

If you go into a professional chef's kitchen you will find that all regularly used equipment and supplies are kept in one spot right where the chef works; prep bowls, spices, knives and so on are all ready at hand. Before their shift, they will have checked the recipes and made sure that all the equipment and supplies they need are prepared and standing by.

In professional kitchens this is called *mis en place* or 'everything in place'. This sensible arrangement can be adapted to cooking in our own kitchens.

When approaching a recipe you have never made before, the first step is to read it all the way through. This ensures there are no surprises ahead. If you don't have every ingredient, find a suitable substitute before you start.

For quick-cooking dishes like stir-fries, prepare all the ingredients beforehand.

Keep your most commonly used ingredients right next to the stove – a selection of salts, dried chilli, sugar and a pepper grinder, for example. Your sauces, spices and condiments should be at hand in a cupboard close by – you don't want to walk miles when you need to add a dash of Worcestershire sauce to a stew.

Instead of a spoon holder I keep a plate next to the stove. All the utensils I use while cooking are placed on it: wooden spoon, tasting spoon, knives and so on. This prevents the counter from becoming cluttered and grubby. When I've finished I pick the plate up with all the utensils and carry it to the sink.

FREEZING FRUIT

Seedless grapes are the essence of summer. But have you ever tried freezing them? Keith discovered this technique when we bought more grapes than we could eat. Wash the grapes and dry them well. Pop them into a container, seal it and freeze. Serve them – still frozen – as a delicious mouth cleanser between courses or just as a frozen snack on a hot day.

Other fruit can also be frozen successfully. For berries, wash and dry them well. Spread the fruit out on a baking tray in one layer and freeze. Once frozen, they can be sealed in a zip lock bag. (To make the quickest ice cream in the world, simply blend frozen fruit with some sugar syrup and cream.)

Do you ever have bananas that are just going over-ripe and you have too many to eat? Put them in the freezer, skin and all. Once frozen, the peel is easily removed and the banana can be eaten as is, or blended with milk for a quick smoothie.

Fruit that is high in natural acids freezes well without discolouring. Mangoes, pineapples, papayas, melons, plums, rhubarb, citrus, guavas and granadillas can all be frozen successfully. Prepare them as if you are going to eat them and then seal in zip lock bags or airtight containers.

With all frozen fruit, it is best to eat it frozen or slightly defrosted, blended or cooked. If allowed to defrost completely, the fruit will be mushy and lose its texture.

FREEZING VEGETABLES

Before freezing vegetables they need to be blanched – this means popping them in boiling water for a short time. Blanching destroys the bacteria that would cause the vegetables to spoil. It also helps retain vitamins and preserves the colour, texture and flavour.

Don't blanch too many vegetables at once; otherwise the water will cool off. Start timing from when the water returns to the boil. Once they have been blanched for the requisite amount of time (see chart on page 236) the vegetables should be plunged into a bowl of ice-cold water to stop them from cooking any further. Prepare a bowl of water with ice cubes and have it standing ready. The vegetables should stay in the water for the same amount of time as they were blanched for.

Drain and dry them well before packing into zip lock bags. Remove the air (see page 238) and seal. If you have a fast-freeze or quick-freeze setting on your fridge, use it, as the quicker the vegetables are frozen the better they will keep.

Vegetable	Preparation	Blanching time
Asparagus	Wash the spears well and cut into bite-sized pieces.	2 minutes
Beans	Wash, top and tail. Cut into pieces about 3 cm long.	3 minutes
Broccoli	Wash and trim into small florets.	3 minutes
Cauliflower	Wash and trim into small florets.	3 minutes
Peas	For ones with edible pods, give them a wash and remove the string from the sides of the pod. For shelling peas, don't wash – just remove them from their pods before blanching.	90 seconds to 2 minutes
Spinach	Choose young leaves and wash well.	2 minutes

PEELING GINGER

The easiest way I have found to peel ginger is to drag the side of a teaspoon over its surface. The skin sloughs off quite easily with the least amount of wastage.

PEELING TOMATOES

Cut an x across the bottom of the tomatoes, just slicing the skin. Place them in a large pot and pour boiling water over them until covered. Leave them for a minute. Lift out with tongs and as soon as they are cool enough to handle, peel the skins off – they will slip off quite easily. If the skins stick at the top central point, use a knife to sever the skin from the flesh.

PREPARING GARLIC

When slicing garlic, you may notice a little green shoot growing inside the cloves. It is called the germ and this is where the new garlic plant will sprout. The older the garlic, the bigger the germ and the more bitter it becomes. If you are using your cloves in a slow cooked dish, don't worry about it, as the bitter taste will dissipate. If you are cooking a quick dish like a stir-fry, rather cut the clove in half and pull the germ out with your fingers or the tip of a knife. For more on peeling and chopping garlic, see page 244.

PREPARING LEMON GRASS

When lemon grass is used whole, it should be bruised first for maximum flavour. Use the handle of a heavy knife and bash it until it flattens. When slicing lemon grass, first peel off the thick outer layers until you reach the pale soft inner flesh. Cut to the required size.

PREPARING HERBS

To remove leaves from a woody stem, hold the stem at its tip. Using two fingers of the other hand, pull downwards to the base, stripping the leaves off in one motion. Break the tip from the stem and add it to the leaves.

To chop herbs evenly, use a sharp

chef's knife. Keep the point at one spot on the surface of the board and using a rocking motion, move in a semi-circle across the pile of leaves. Keep one hand over the back of the knife to steady it.

Keep pushing the uncut herbs to the centre until they are all evenly chopped.

Herbs can also be sliced into fine ribbons or *chiffonade*. Stack herb leaves such as basil or mint evenly into a pile. Roll the pile lengthways into a long cigar. Starting at the pointed end of the leaf, finely slice the cigar into thin slices, which will form delicate herb ribbons.

PREPARING LEMONS, LIMES AND OTHER CITRUS

To squeeze the most juice out of citrus fruit, drop it on the floor and roll it with your foot. This breaks up the cells and releases the juice more easily.

My friend Michael, who lives in Berlin, showed me the most practical way to

cut lemons. Whenever I cut them using this method, I think of him.

Cut in half horizontally and then vertically into quarters. Cut each quarter vertically again. Place on its horizontal cut side with the pointed end facing up. Slice the white pithy section off, taking the pips with it.

PREPARING MANGOES

Cut two parallel slices down the flat side of the pip, cutting as close to the pip as you can.

Cut an even criss-cross pattern into the flesh, cutting down to the skin but not through it. Use your thumbs to turn the sides inside out, so the cut sections stick out.

Either eat it just like this, or cut the cubes off the skin, cutting as close to the skin as possible. Peel the remaining centre section and dice the flesh off the pip.

PREPARING ONIONS

Wetting an onion first makes peeling easier. If you are using only a portion of onion, do not peel the whole thing. Cut off just the amount you need and the remainder will last longer with its peel on.

When cutting onions, use your sharpest knife. Cut the stem end off the peeled onion. Then cut a small section off one side of the onion, to create a flat surface so the onion doesn't roll.

Place the flat side on a board and slice in rings to the thickness required until you are nearly at the root end. Lay it flat and continue slicing until you reach the thickened root section, which is then discarded.

To cut evenly diced squares, prepare as above and place the flat side on a board. Cut parallel horizontal slices (from stem to root) into the onion, but don't cut all the way through to the root. Then cut vertical slices, the same thickness as the horizontal slices.

REMOVING AIR FROM ZIP LOCK BAGS

If you have a vacuum pack machine — lucky you. If not, use this simple method to remove air from zip locks before sealing them.

Pop a straw into the zip lock and seal the edges around the straw. Suck the air out with the straw until the plastic seals tightly around the contents.

If sealing a liquid, suck until a little bit of liquid comes up the straw. Pull the straw out and as soon as it is clear of the lock, seal it tightly.

ROASTING PINE NUTS

Heat up a cast iron pan over medium-high heat. Add the pine nuts and leave on the heat for a minute or two. As soon as they begin to brown, give the pan a shake and leave for a further minute or so.

Once they are nicely browned, remove from the pan immediately, otherwise they will continue to cook.

ROASTING SPICES

When spices are dry-roasted or fried in a little oil, their essential oils are released, enhancing and boosting the flavour of a dish.

Follow the same procedure as for toasting pine nuts. If you add some oil to the pan, it will be strongly flavoured with the roasted spice.

SALTING EGGPLANT

Put the cut eggplant into a colander set over a bowl. Sprinkle liberally with salt, tossing the eggplant pieces so they are evenly coated. Leave to stand for half an hour, while the bitter juices are released. Rinse very well and pat dry.

STERILISING BOTTLES

Before sterilising, wash the bottles and lids in hot soapy water and rinse well. If you are using bottles with screw-top lids, place them upside-down on an oven-proof tray, so that any water drains out. Place the lids alongside the bottles on the tray. Bake at 160° C for at least 10 minutes. Remove them from the oven one by one as you fill them.

An alternative method to the oven is to place the washed, wet bottles upside-down in a microwave on high for 3 minutes. Be careful when handling hot jars – they can hurt you!

If you are using bottles with rubber rings, place the bottles, lids and rings on a rack in a deep pot. Cover with water and bring to the boil, then simmer for 10 minutes. Remove with tongs and place on a tray covered with a clean dishcloth to drip dry.

You need to sterilise the jug or ladle you use for pouring sauces or preserves into the bottles. This is best done by boiling them in hot water for 10 minutes.

STIR-FRYING

This is a very healthy way to cook food, especially vegetables. Using minimal oil, no water and a speedy cooking process, stir-frying retains nutrients in the food and preserves a fresh colour too. For best results, heat your wok first and then add the oil. Cut your ingredients into evenly-sized pieces and dry them well – wet vegetables will steam, not fry.

STORING GREENS IN THE FRIDGE

The best way to store lettuces, Asian greens or any other leafy greens in the fridge is to put them in a zip lock bag lined with a paper towel. Blow some air in with a straw and then seal it quickly. The air cushion not only keeps them fresh, but prevents them from being crushed.

THICKENING SAUCES

If you add flour to a hot liquid you will land up with a horribly lumpy sauce full of balls of raw-tasting flour. Yuk.

When flour hits the hot liquid, the starch molecules clump together and the outside ones expand, forming a barrier, which stops the liquid reaching inside.

To prevent this from happening, the starch molecules need to be separated first, so that when they meet the hot liquid they can each expand and, in the process, thicken the sauce.

There are four ways of doing this:

1. Make a thin paste of flour mixed with cold liquid before adding it to hot liquid.

2. Sprinkle flour into a pan of meat and vegetables and mix it into the fat, cooking it before slowly adding any liquid.

3. Make a *roux* by mixing equal quantities of fat (oil or butter) and flour together and cooking it. Liquid is then added very slowly, while being stirred constantly. The cooking time of the *roux* varies from a few minutes (eliminating the raw taste of the flour) to more than 20 minutes, resulting in a deep brown mixture that adds a toasted, nutty flavour to the sauce.

4. Make a *beurre manié* (French for kneaded butter) of flour and butter mixed together in equal proportions. By kneading the fat and the flour together well, each starch molecule is separated by a layer of fat. When a lump of *beurre manié* is added to a sauce, the molecules separate and swell, thickening the sauce. It is great for making a quick gravy. It makes sauces glossy and enriches them with butter. However, only small amounts should be used, otherwise the sauce can taste too floury. Mix chicken fat (scooped off the top of chicken stock) with flour in equal proportions to create a *beurre manié* with an added punch of flavour. Store it

in a sealed jar in the freezer.

Of the above methods, the least tasty is the first, often resulting in a raw, flour-flavoured sauce. Making a *roux* is the tastiest and most common method. The second and the third methods are very similar – in the second method you are essentially mixing a *roux* with the vegetables and meat; while the last method is the quickest and is best to use when making a quick gravy or sauce.

TARTING UP A WHITE SAUCE

When I make a white sauce (also know as a *béchamel* sauce), I often add aromatic ingredients such as paprika or fresh herbs to the butter before mixing in the flour. Purist white sauce makers will probably frown upon this, but it makes sense to me to flavour it at this stage. Instead of it just being a white sauce, it becomes something far more interesting.

TESTING TO SEE WHEN JAMS AND JELLIES ARE READY

If you have a sugar thermometer, use it to test the temperature – when it reaches 105°C (in other words, 5° above the boiling point of water), it is ready. If you don't have a thermometer, use the 'wrinkle' method. Place a saucer in the freezer. Dollop a small amount of the jam or jelly onto the icy saucer and leave it for about a minute. Push it with your finger and if it has formed a slight skin, which wrinkles as you push, it is ready.

GADGET GIRL

I am a sucker for gadgets. I am always impressed by someone demonstrating a whiz-bang gizmo that professes to make my life easier. However, more than half of the ones I am seduced into buying land up gathering dust at the back of the top shelf. Despite using them a couple of times, I always land up returning to the basics. Here are a few of my favourite things.

BAKING STONE

Also called a pizza stone, these terracotta discs are fantastic for baking bread and pizza.

When not using it for direct cooking, store the baking stone on the bottom of the oven where it will help maintain an even temperature for all other baking.

When cooking oily dough, such as pizza, directly on the stone, cover it with aluminium foil. Terracotta is very absorbent and will soak up the oil, which will then burn.

BOWLS

Collect a range of different sized prep bowls; from small ones for chopped garlic, chilli and ginger, to larger ones for diced vegetables.

CAST IRON PANS

Many years ago, when my Aunt Bee retired and moved from Johannesburg, she gave me a set of cast iron pans. I wasn't a keen cook back then so they were stuck in the back of a cupboard and forgotten. Years later I discovered them and excitedly pulled them out. They looked rather neglected, with brown rusty patches. I quickly learnt how to season them and brought back their lustre and gloss. Now I can't cook without them.

It is worth investing in some cast iron cookware – it will last you a lifetime (probably a few!) and is wonderful to cook on. Heavy cast iron distributes heat evenly and retains it for a long time. It can be used on the stovetop and in the oven. And food does not stick to a well-seasoned pan. Cast iron is a healthy option, as studies are now showing that pans with a chemically created non-stick surface could be harmful to us – especially once it starts wearing off.

By 'seasoning' your cast iron cookware, I mean filling any gaps in the metal with oil and cooking it in. This protects the metal from rusting and makes the surface smooth and non-stick.

Before using your new cast iron pan, wash it in hot, soapy water. Rub a layer of vegetable oil all over – inside and out. If it has a cast iron lid, rub oil onto that too. Heat your oven to 180° C. Place the lid and pan upside down on the top shelf with a baking tray underneath to catch any drippings. Bake for an hour and then leave to cool.

To look after your cast iron cookware, wash it gently by hand. Don't use a dishwasher as this will remove the seasoning. Make sure it is absolutely dry before storing. If you use it regularly, you won't need to keep oiling it, but if not, oil it before storing. Leave it out in the sun for half an hour to make sure it is completely dry and, while still warm, rub it with oil, wiping off any excess with a paper towel. In humid climates, store your pots with the lids off to prevent moisture from gathering.

CUTTING BOARDS

It might seem an obvious gadget, but a good cutting board can make the difference between a meditative chopping session and a chore. I like wooden boards that can be used on either side and are the kindest to knife edges. I have a selection of boards so I don't cross contaminate my fruit with chillies or garlic. I regularly rub my boards with olive oil so they don't dry out and split.

FOOD PROCESSOR, BLENDER OR SMALL CHOPPER

Any of these are useful aids for busy chefs, enabling them to quickly chop, dice, blend or purée. There are many different varieties on the market, so choose one that best suits your budget and needs.

FLOUR SHAKER

I use this simple implement every time I add flour to a hot pan. It distributes the flour evenly and reduces the chances of lumps forming.

GARLIC CHOPPER

This is probably the most well-used device in my kitchen. I am not a great fan of a garlic crusher, as the resulting garlic is too squashed for my liking. My Alligator garlic chopper has a razor-sharp stainless steel grid that produces square dice cuts with a simple one-push action. The uniform squares result in more flavour when cooking, as there is more surface area to brown.

I also use it to dice small onions, ginger and even chillies. (I bought mine at a kitchen shop. If you can't find one locally – look online.)

GARLIC PEELER

When I first saw these silicone tubes they were selling at a ridiculous price – but I bought one anyway as I had read about them in my American cooking magazines. I was glad I did because it was every bit as practical as the reviews had promised. A year or so later I found them at the 'R5 Store' in Brixton. I bought dozens and gave everybody garlic peelers for Christmas.

IMMERSION BLENDER

These stick blenders are invaluable for making smooth soups. Always remove the pot from the heat before using it and blend using short bursts – this prevents splashing. Make sure the entire head of the blender is immersed in the liquid before turning it on otherwise hot liquid will explode out.

JULIENNE PEELER

This peeler creates perfect strips of carrots and other vegetables. It is a great gadget – so simple, yet it does the job it was designed to do perfectly.

KNIVES

If you ask any chef what their favourite implement is, most will probably tell you it's their knife. I bought my first proper chef's knife when I was travelling through the United States in 1994 and I still use it today. A good knife is expensive but will last ages if looked after properly. Only use the blade for cutting. When you sweep ingredients off a cutting board, turn the knife upside down and use the back – not the blade.

Don't keep your knives loose in a drawer; use a sheath or a knife stand. Cut on a wooden or composite plastic cutting board only – don't use ceramic, glass, marble or steel boards as they will harm the blade.

And be sure to sharpen your blade regularly with a good-quality sharpener.

LEMON ZESTER

I love using use lemon (and other citrus) zest when I cook. For years I used a peeler and then cut the peel into strips – until I bought a dedicated lemon zester. It is far more efficient, much quicker and produces fine strips of zest.

MEASURING CUPS, SPOONS AND KITCHEN SCALES

In most of my recipes I have used simple units of measurement based on teaspoons (5 ml), tablespoons (15 ml) and cups (250 ml). However, if you are going to be doing any baking, a good kitchen scale is essential.

With most other recipes you can get away with estimating the ingredients, but with baking it pays to follow the recipe!

I bought a set of stainless steel measuring cups and spoons many years ago and they still look as good as new. I like stainless steel as it is hygienic and it lasts forever.

Nested measuring cups save storage space and spoons on a ring are kept conveniently together. I also have a large glass measuring jug which is useful for anything over one cup.

The kitchen scale of my childhood was a far cry from today's modern digital ones. Mom's scale had brass bowls on either side, resembling the scales of justice. Metal discs of different sizes, inscribed with their weight, were added to one side, totalling up the exact pound and ounce.

Ingredients were carefully added to the opposite side, until the two bowls balanced.

Today's scales are not nearly as romantic – but they are just as essential. If you are planning to do any baking, invest a good kitchen scale.

PAPER TOWELS

These are endlessly useful in the kitchen. Apart from using them for wiping, mopping and drying, I place them next to my cutting board to catch the vegetable offcuts and peels and then pop the whole thing into my compost-collecting bin.

PESTLE AND MORTAR

The most treasured items in my kitchen are my pestle and mortars. The one is made of yellowwood and was turned by my grandfather who lived to nearly 105.

The other is from my father who is a retired pharmacist. It is made from white porcelain and the pestle has a wooden handle. It was the one he used for many years to mix prescriptions, in the days when pharmacists still made up their own pills. It is tough and durable and I use it to grind roast spices and harder ingredients.

I use my grandfather's wooden one for grinding fresh herbs, garlic and other softer ingredients.

Although it is easier to resort to the food processor when blending ingredients, there is a wonderful subtle texture resulting from a pestle and mortar that a food processor is too quick to achieve.

RICE COOKER

I was busy cooking one evening when the phone rang. It was an old friend and soon we were deep in conversation. I forgot all about the rice boiling on the stove.

It became so hot that when I finally remembered and grabbed the pot off the heat, the metal base had melted and stuck to the burner – liquid strands of molten metal were all that connected it to the pot.

On my next visit to Thailand, I brought a rice cooker back home with me. It is a magic gadget, as it not only cooks rice to perfection, but it keeps it warm for ages without drying it out – perfect for dinner parties. And I'll never burn the rice again.

However, you don't have to go to Thailand to buy one; they are now readily available at any Asian supermarket.

SPICE GRINDER

Whole spices retain their flavour far longer then pre-ground ones. I keep a couple of empty spice grinders in my cupboard (one for sweet and one for spicy) for grinding whole spices such as cloves, coriander and cumin.

TONGS

A good pair of tongs is essential. I use them for flipping things over, fishing hot food out of water and when working with any hot oil.

I have a bamboo pair and a pop-open stainless steel pair with a silicone grip end. The bamboo pair is ideal for smaller items. The silicone ones look groovy and don't scratch pans.

WOK

If you want to get serious about cooking Asian food you will need a wok. There are many different varieties on the market. They all work best on a gas hob as this gives you high temperatures with the flexibility of instant adjustment of heat. If you have an electric stove, rather choose a flat-bottomed wok. Non-stick varieties are fine for sautéing but not for stir-frying at high temperatures. My favourite wok is a traditional Chinese thin cast iron one. It heats up quickly, it is well seasoned (see page 243) so it is non-stick and it is light and easy to use. Oh – and it was inexpensive. A lid is useful for keeping food hot when you have finished cooking or when bringing a soup to the boil.

WOODEN SPOONS AND SPATULAS

When one of my wooden spoons split in two, Keith sanded the edges down and the result is one of my most useful implements.

I keep a variety of shapes and sizes of wooden spoons and spatulas next to my stove and use them for stirring, stir-frying and sautéing everything.

Fast becoming my favourites, bamboo spatulas are long lasting, durable and stronger than wood. Bamboo is a highly renewable resource so they are also an eco-friendly option.

INGREDIENTS

ALCOHOL

Adding a well-rounded red wine to a winter stew will contribute to its flavour in more ways than one. Alcohol enhances the flavours of food because of two factors: evaporation and molecular bonding.

Firstly, alcohol is volatile, meaning it evaporates rapidly. When you add it to a dish it carries the flavours to the nose, enhancing the taste sensation. (Think about how tasteless food is when you have a cold!)

Secondly, most aromatics, such as herbs, garlic and other seasonings, only dissolve in fat but most ingredients consist primarily of water. We all know that fat and water don't mix and this is where the magic of alcohol comes in: one end of an alcohol molecule can combine with fats and the other end bonds with water.

When you add alcohol to a dish, it carries flavours into the meat and vegetables. This works particularly well when you add alcohol to a marinade. Even if you use flavourless vodka, it will still help enhance the taste.

And contrary to what many believe, alcohol does not 'burn off' during cooking. With a flambé, for example, 75% of the alcohol is retained and if you cook a long slow stew, about 25% will still be there. (Thanks to *Fine Cooking* magazine for enlightening me on these scientific foodie facts.)

ASIAN LIME

This citrus tree also goes by the unfortunate name of kaffir lime. The *Citrus hystrix* is native to Southeast Asia where its name does not have the same offensive connotations as it does here. Its distinctive double leaf adds a unique citrus flavour to many Asian dishes. For several years only dried leaves were available in South Africa but with the tree now available at a few nurseries, more and more greengrocers are supplying fresh leaves.

BLACK GOLD

Professional chefs make thick, sweet balsamic reductions by slow cooking balsamic vinegar with various seasonings. Black Gold is a delicious locally made reduction – available from markets and delis.

Since I started using Black Gold to make salad dressing, I hardly ever use anything else.

COCONUT MILK

Coconut milk is not the water from the centre of the coconut; it is made from the white flesh. Different makes vary in flavour and thickness – look for those made in Thailand and try to find preservative-free brands.

You can make your own by mixing desiccated coconut with an equal amount of hot water. Leave to soak for half an hour and then start squeezing the mixture with your hands until the liquid becomes thick and 'coconutty'. Strain it through cheesecloth – this 'first pressing' makes the richest coconut milk. For a thinner second pressing, soak the coconut again and repeat the process.

I always keep a couple of packets of coconut powder in my pantry. If I don't need a whole can of coconut milk or cream in a recipe, it is easier to add the required amount using the powder mixed with water. If you don't use a whole can, store it in a sealed container in the freezer.

DRIED BEANS

If you have been put off using dried beans by having to soak them for hours before cooking – there is a quicker method. Rinse the beans a few times, discarding any floaters. Put them in a large pot, adding 4 cups of water per 1 cup of beans. Bring the water to the boil and reduce heat to a simmer for about 10 minutes. Remove from the heat, cover and leave for about an hour.

They are now ready to be cooked.

There are a couple of 'dried bean rules' that are useful to know. Acidic ingredients such as lemon, tomatoes, wine or vinegar prevent beans from softening, so only add them after the beans are already tender.

Sugar inhibits softening – this is why a dish such as Yosemite baked beans and pork (page 218) can be cooked for such a long time with the beans still retaining their texture and shape. Salt helps to soften tough skins, so if you have an old batch of dried beans, try soaking them in salted water before you cook them.

FRIED GARLIC AND ONION

Available at Asian supermarkets, these tasty, crunchy bits add an instant hit of flavour to a meal. Keep in the fridge once open and use within a few weeks. To make your own, see page 29.

GALANGAL

Although it looks similar to ginger, galangal tastes completely different. It has a complex, earthy flavour with an almost lemony tang, and is used in cuisines throughout Southeast Asia. It is mostly available dried or powdered but as it becomes more widely known, fresh roots are starting to appear in Asian greengrocers. Also available is galangal bottled in brine, which holds its flavour pretty well.

JAPANESE CHILLI

Its Japanese name, *shichimi togarashi,* means seven flavours.

This wonderful spice mix contains chilli pepper, roasted orange peel, yellow and black sesame seeds, Japanese pepper, seaweed, and ginger.

It is readily available from Asian supermarkets. I use it whenever I want to add a bit of bite as well as subtle additional flavouring to a dish.

KETJAP MANIS

A thick, dark Indonesian soy sauce that is sweeter and more complex in taste than ordinary soy sauce. It is great added to any Asian stir-fry, marinade or soup, adding much more flavour than ordinary soy sauce does.

MIRIN

Available from Asian supermarkets, mirin is a low-alcohol, sweet, rice wine used extensively in Japanese cooking. I often add it to a dish that needs slight sweetening. It helps enhance flavours and is especially good in any fish dish.

OLIVE OIL

Olive oil has been used for thousands of years and is one of the main components of a healthy Mediterranean diet. I use olive oil extensively in my cooking.

The labelling of olive oil can be confusing: what do 'extra virgin' and 'cold-pressed' actually mean? In general, these labels serve as a guide to the quality of the oil and refer to the method of extraction.

Virgin means that no chemicals and only mechanical methods were used to extract the oil from the olives.

Extra virgin is the highest-grade olive oil. The 'extra' can be added to the labels of virgin oils (mechanically extracted) only if they have less than 0.8% free oleic acid and are of superior taste, colour and aroma.

These are the most expensive oils and are best used in salad dressings and for dipping sauces where their full flavour can be savoured.

Cold-pressed means that the temperatures in the processing mills were kept below 27° C during extraction.

Refined means that chemicals were used in the extraction process, thereby increasing the amount of oil yielded by the olives.

Pure olive oil, **olive oil** or **light olive oil** are all blends of virgin oil and refined oil. These oils are less expensive and less flavourful, and should be used only for cooking.

Pomace oil is extracted from pomace, the ground olive flesh and pits that remain after extraction. The remnants of oil are obtained by treating the pomace with solvents.

It is not recommended for human consumption and is best used on your hair and body.

PALM SUGAR

Also know as *jaggery*, palm sugar is made from the sap of palm trees. It tastes of molasses and has a richer flavour and is healthier for us than cane sugar.

In Burma we spent a day with a family who makes *jaggery*. Twice a day the farmer nimbly climbs his trees to collect the translucent white syrup. Some of it is fermented to make *toddy*, a sweet alcoholic drink, some is distilled to make a way more lethal concoction and the rest is boiled down to make *jaggery*.

I use palm sugar extensively in all my Asian soups and curries. You can buy it in round 'cakes' at most Asian supermarkets and it keeps for ages.

It is quite hard and if you use a knife to cut it, chunks go flying all over the place. Use a grater instead.

POMEGRANATE CONCENTRATE

A combination of tart and sweet, pomegranate concentrate is delicious in salad dressings. You can find it at most branches of Woolies and some delis.

SAKE

A Japanese wine made from fermented rice. Light, dry and refreshing, sake is not only great to drink, it is also a delicious ingredient to add to Asian soups and sauces.

SESAME SEEDS

Black seeds are available at Asian supermarkets. They taste the same as the white ones but add a visual zing to a dish. Sesame seeds add a crunch as well as a nutty flavour to a meal.

SHRIMP PASTE

I am allergic to fresh shrimps, but luckily I can eat dried and fermented ones, as this pungent paste, made from ground-up fermented shrimps, is found in almost every curry paste throughout Southeast Asia.

It is available from Asian and other supermarkets.

SOY SAUCE

Dark soy sauce is thicker and stronger than light soy sauce. Use dark soy sauce for cooking and light for marinades, sauces and dressings. There are many brands available in supermarkets – try to find a preservative-free sauce without artificial flavour enhancers (like MSG).

SWEET CHILLI SAUCE

This sweet, hot garlicky condiment is used extensively in Thai cuisine. It is available from most supermarkets as well as Asian supermarkets. For my recipe see page 94. It is one of my favourite ingredients and I don't think I could cook without it. I use it in marinades, to make sauces, to add vigour to a simple soup, as well as on its own as a delicious dipping sauce.

TAMARIND LIQUID

Made from the sweet and sour fruit of the tamarind tree, this is one of the main souring ingredients in Thai cooking. It is sold in blocks at Asian supermarkets. To make tamarind liquid, place 2 tablespoons of tamarind paste in a bowl. Pour half a cup of boiling water over it and leave to soak for 20 minutes. Mash the paste into the water with a spoon and then strain the liquid from the pulp. I use it to add an unusual acidic tang to many Asian dishes.

TERIYAKI SAUCE

Teriyaki is a Japanese word that refers to a method of cooking involving grilling and glazing with a sauce. Teriyaki sauce is made from sugar, cornflour, garlic, sake, mirin and soy sauce. It is available from many Asian and other supermarkets. Apart from its traditional use as a glazing sauce, it is perfect for making a quick marinade or adding to stir-fried vegetables.

VERJUICE

Literally meaning 'green juice', verjuice is the unfermented juice of semi-ripe grapes. It is acidic, but not nearly as sharp as either vinegar or lemon juice. I mostly use it in marinades and particularly for salad dressings and sauces.

RECIPE INDEX